THE SUPER CREW'S BREAKFAST COOKBOOK FOR KIDS

50 TASTY RECIPES
+ 100 FUN NUTRITION ACTIVITIES

MELISSA HALAS, MA, RDN, CDE

Visit SuperKidsNutrition.com
For more fun, healthy & tasty ideas!

For my daughter, Abigail - your beautiful spirit is always abundant in love, encouragement, and care. Your positivity inspires me every day.

ALLERGY INFORMATION

GLUTEN-FREE

NUT-FREE

PEANUT-FREE

Any recipe that has one or more of these icons will not contain these allergens or will offer a substitution in the ingredient list for the allergen.

		GF	NF	PF

MEASURING GUIDE

Note these abbreviations for the ingredient amounts:

tsp. = teaspoon(s)

Tbsp. = tablespoon(s)

oz. = ounce(s)

lb. = pound

TABLE OF CONTENTS – ACTIVITIES

DEAR READER,

Many of these activities are meant to be enjoyed as a family or in a group. Encourage children to ask for your help along the way.

Take turns reading the sections out loud and help your kids complete the more challenging parts of the activities. Choose a new recipe each week to try together!

See SuperKidsNutrition.com/SuperCrewBreakfastBook to:

- learn how to use this as a parent, teacher, or health educator

- gain guidance into introducing new foods, food preparation tips, time savers, food allergy substitutions, and more

- search for answers together with our hints, clues and helpful links

- access this book's supplemental content

While you're on the website, visit our Tools and Resources section for the Super Crew's age-specific printable cooking guide to help determine what your kids can do in the kitchen.

The Super Crew's pets include Cinnamon (the dog), Pinkie (the fish), Quack (the duck), and Flutter (the butterfly), and they make appearances throughout the book. They are hidden and in plain site. Have your little ones discover and circle them as they work through the book.

You'll find the answer key for all of the activities at the back of the book. This is also where you'll discover how many times the pets appear in the book.

Have fun cooking and learning about nutrition together with the Super Crew!

♥ The Super Crew ♥
&
Melissa

Meet the SUPER CREW

SUPER BABY ABIGAIL

KIRA

TOM-TOM

JESSIE

CINNAMON THE DOG

PINKIE THE FISH

MARCUS

PENNY

CARLOS

ANDY

QUACK THE DUCK

FLUTTER THE BUTTERFLY

Kids are often labeled as picky eaters when in reality, their taste development is still "under construction." As they grow, develop, and explore new foods, they will naturally learn to enjoy many foods and will likely pass on others (just like adults!). Try not to influence your kids with your own food prejudices. Your children may love Brussels sprouts, while you turn your nose up at them. You may love sweet, while they love savory! Use this as a guide to help your kids try new healthy foods without force or pressure. Be sure to get in on the action, and role model your willingness to explore new foods and flavors. And remember, patience is key. Healthy eating development happens with encouragement and consistency, not in an instant or overnight.

Fickleness: They may love bananas this week but by next week tell you they never really liked bananas. Don't go bananas! Kids' taste preferences change.

Sweetness: Kids have varying preferences for sweetness, and this will change throughout infancy and childhood. Babies love the taste of sugar, and nature accommodates them with sweet tasting mom's milk. For foods such as yogurt or oatmeal, start with just a drizzle of natural sweetener (honey, agave or maple syrup, etc.) and add a bit more as needed.

Savory: Kids may surprise you and ask for bold, savory flavors. Bland doesn't always mean better! Try spicing things up with some new herbs, a squeeze of lemon or lime, a splash of hot sauce, or go bold with new and interesting ethnic cuisines.

Texture: Your child may say they hate tomato sauce, but perhaps it's just too chunky. Try serving foods in different forms such as chunky, puréed, chopped, raw, cooked, shredded, or spiralized into "noodles". This process may be a bit slow, but over time, the variety and exposure will result in an expanded palate. Asking your child to describe the food can help as well. You can even make it a fun game at the grocery store by having them select a new food based on its color, size, or shape!

Shape: Your kids may not like chopped cucumber, but like it julienne style – perfect for dips! Or, the way you're cutting up their sandwich just isn't doing it. Next time cut the bread horizontally instead of vertically. Cookie cutters are a fun way to cut shapes out of melon slices, length-sliced zucchini slices, or cheese wedges.

Temperature: Your child may hate cooked corn and peas, fresh raspberries or cold yogurt. There's a possible quick solution! Try serving corn, peas, and raspberries frozen, right out of the freezer. Check your produce company's guidelines. Some recommend for frozen produce to be cooked or microwaved to 165°F for at least 15 seconds before served to prevent food-borne illness. Heat the fruit in the microwave, and mix with their yogurt to warm it up. Try toasted nuts, or frozen smoothie pops! Once again, variety is key!

Size & Timing: We know that real babies are tiny, adorable, and lovable. The same thing goes for food - try baby bean burgers, petite potatoes, baby tomatoes, etc. Smaller portion sizes are less intimidating. You also want your kids to show up to meals hungry, so timing is key! As much as possible, adhere to a meal and snack schedule, and discourage all-day bites and grazing. Three meals and 1-2 scheduled snacks will help promote healthy eating development.

Meal Plan: If you involve your kids in the process, they will feel ownership in menu planning and will start off each meal with a couple of items that they know they like. Letting them make decisions about food lets them know that their voice is heard! When kids feel in charge, they are more likely to experience new foods on their own terms.

Get more tips on SuperKidsNutrition.com.

They are foods that grow in nature, like fruit, veggies, beans, whole grains, nuts, seeds, herbs, and spices.

Plant foods have superpowers from things called phytonutrients. We call them "fight-o-nutrients" because they fight off invasion from bacteria, viruses, and disease so each plant can survive and grow strong.

You can't get these fight-o-nutrients in a pill. You need to get them from the plant food so all the plant compounds can work together. Plants also provide us with vitamins and minerals that are needed for activities our bodies perform every day.

PLANT-BASED FOOD POWER!

The same plant fight-o-nutrients that protect plants protect people too!
Check off all the boosts you want for your body from plant foods:

☐ Good health
☐ Grow big and strong
☐ Fight off diseases, germs, and bacteria
☐ Energy
☐ Protect body cells

☐ Healthy skin, hair, and nails
☐ Protect your brain, heart, and lungs
☐ Prevent many types of cancer
☐ Better digestion (easier to poop!)

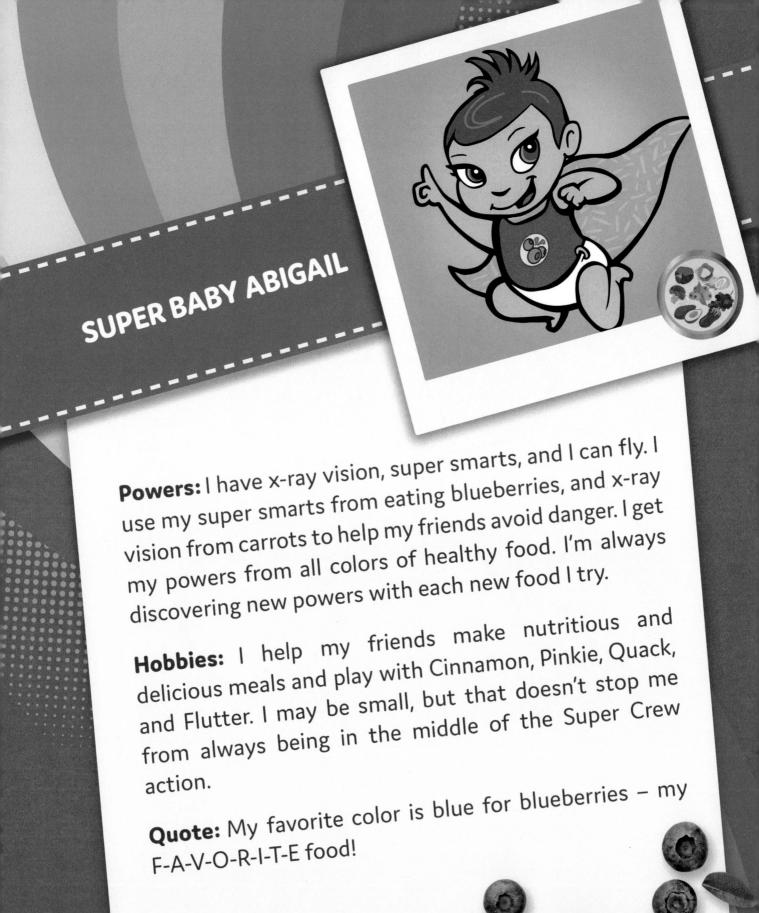

SUPER BABY ABIGAIL

Powers: I have x-ray vision, super smarts, and I can fly. I use my super smarts from eating blueberries, and x-ray vision from carrots to help my friends avoid danger. I get my powers from all colors of healthy food. I'm always discovering new powers with each new food I try.

Hobbies: I help my friends make nutritious and delicious meals and play with Cinnamon, Pinkie, Quack, and Flutter. I may be small, but that doesn't stop me from always being in the middle of the Super Crew action.

Quote: My favorite color is blue for blueberries – my F-A-V-O-R-I-T-E food!

COZY APPLE CARROT STREUSEL MUFFIN CUPS

Makes 8-10 muffins

Ingredients:

- 1½ cups old-fashioned rolled oats
- ⅓ cup ground flax meal
- ½ small apple, shredded
- ½ medium carrot, grated
- 1 egg
- 2 Tbsp. honey or maple syrup
- 1⅓ cups plain nonfat or low-fat unsweetened milk of your choice (we used soy milk)
- 1 tsp. vanilla extract
- 2 tsp. cinnamon
- ¼ tsp. nutmeg
- 1 tsp. baking powder
- ¼ cup dried cranberries, plus more for topping
- ¼ cup pecans, chopped, plus more for topping
- Greek yogurt, honey or vegan butter spread, for topping only

Directions:

1. Preheat oven to 350°F.
2. Line a muffin tin and grease with oil or butter.
3. Combine all of the ingredients (except yogurt) in a large mixing bowl.
4. Once fully mixed, spoon the batter evenly into the muffin tins, filling each cup to the top.
5. Bake for 20-25 minutes, until muffins spring when touched and are lightly browned on top.
6. Let cool, top each muffin with two spoons of yogurt, sprinkle with a few cranberries and pecans, and enjoy.

I like eating my morning oatmeal baked like a muffin.

FRUITY BLUEBERRY SMOOTHIE

Makes 3 servings

Ingredients:

- 2 cups frozen unsweetened blueberries (do not thaw)
- ½-1 cup orange juice (OJ)
- ½ cup water (if only ½ cup of OJ used)
- ¾ cup plain nonfat or low-fat unsweetened yogurt
- ½ medium frozen banana
- ½ tsp. pure vanilla extract

Directions:

1. Place blueberries, orange juice (and water if choosing ½ and ½), yogurt, banana and vanilla extract in the blender container.
2. Cover securely and blend for 30-35 seconds or until thick and smooth. For thinner smoothies, add more juice. For thicker smoothies, add more frozen fruit.
3. Pour into 3 glasses and serve.

HAVE A "BLUE TOOTH" CONTEST. EAT FROZEN BLUEBERRIES TOGETHER, SMILE, AND SEE WHO HAS THE BLUEST TEETH.

I love picking a basket of blueberries at the farmers market.

VERY BERRY APPLE BREAKFAST PIE

Makes 5-6 servings

Ingredients:

- 2-3 apples
- 2 tsp. cinnamon
- 2 tsp. honey
- 2 cups frozen mixed berries
- 1 cup granola or homemade oat topping (see list below) or use GF granola
- 1 tsp. olive oil
- ¼ cup walnuts
- Dollop of Greek yogurt

Homemade oat topping:

- ¾ cup oats
- ¼ cup whole-wheat flour or GF oat flour
- 3 Tbsp. olive oil
- 1-2 Tbsp. honey

Directions:

1. Preheat oven to 350°F and lightly grease a pie dish with olive oil.
2. Thinly slice the apples with an adult. Coat apple slices with honey and cinnamon.
3. In alternating layers, place the sliced apples and mixed berries in your pie dish.
4. If you chose the home-made oat topping, combine all of the oat topping ingredients in a medium bowl and mix well, then add it to the top of your pie. If using pre-made granola, add it to the top *after* baking the pie.
5. Bake for 35-45 minutes, or until apples are tender.
6. Remove from the oven and let cool. Then, slice into portions, put in small bowls, and top with a dollop of Greek yogurt and walnuts.
7. Enjoy this tasty morning treat and keep the leftovers in the fridge!

HOW TO GROW BLUEBERRIES

This is an activity to do with an adult.

1. Buy a seed, seedling, or small bush.
2. Choose a sunny location with well-drained soil, a big pot, or a raised bed. Plant your future blueberry bush in an acid loving soil mixture, like a half mixture of peat moss and planting mix.
3. Once the plant is growing well, use acid fertilizers like rhododendron or azalea formulations. Water well after fertilizing. You can also make your own low-cost fertilizer by adding two tablespoons of vinegar to a gallon of water.

How to pick and store your blueberry crop:

• Ready to pick your blueberries? A ripe blueberry should look all blue with a silver, powdery look, and have no yellow or green spots. It should be firm to touch.

• Rinse them well just before serving. They taste best if you eat them right away but you can keep them in the fridge for up to 5 days.

COLORING FUN!

Blueberries give me super smarts.

DRAWING ACTIVITY
Directions: Draw your blueberry garden below. You can put them in pots, in the ground, or on a raised bed!

FACTS ABOUT BLUEBERRIES

Directions: Underline the word blueberry or blueberries when reading the facts below. Circle words you don't know and look them up in the online dictionary.

1. Frozen blueberries taste great, cost less, last longer, and are yummy eaten frozen or warm.
2. Blueberries have anthocyanins (antho-sigh-ah-nins), a type of plant compound that's good for your heart and brain.
3. Anthocyanins are one of the Super Crew's favorite phytonutrients or what they call "fight-o-nutrients," because they help fight off diseases.
4. The darker the blueberry, the more antioxidant superpowers they have.
5. Wild blueberries contain 40% more antioxidant potential than cultivated varieties.

Pretend you grow lots of blueberries….

What kind of blueberries did you grow? Do you want tiny and sweet, or big and round? Visit the farmers market or garden store to learn which type to grow. How will you sell your blueberries? At a farmers market, to friends and families, or to someone else? How much will your blueberries cost? Will anyone get a discount? Discuss this with a family member or friend or write your thoughts on a piece of paper.

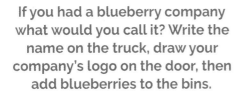

If you had a blueberry company what would you call it? Write the name on the truck, draw your company's logo on the door, then add blueberries to the bins.

COLORING FUN!

CREATE YOUR OWN SMOOTHIE STORE!

Directions: Give your store some color! What colors go best with your store name? Use them below!

If you had your own famous smoothie store, what would you name it?

Have your family members or friends come up with their own store names below.

Have everyone vote for the best name and write it below!

COLORING FUN!

ACTIVITY

HELP SUPER BABY ABIGAIL GET THROUGH THE EYE MAZE!

Eggs have fight-o-nutrients called lutein and zeaxanthin that help you see better! This is because the chickens who lay the eggs eat plant-based foods with these compounds. Find your way through the maze with Super Baby Abigail to the center of the pupil to get x-ray vision just like her!

START HERE

END HERE

Lutein (loo-teen) and **zeaxanthin** (zee-uh-zan-thin) are types of fight-o-nutrients called carotenoids.

Which vitamin family do carotenoids (lutein and zeaxanthin) belong to?

Hint: *It's a vitamin that's good for your eyes.*

Vitamin A
Vitamin B
Vitamin C

THE SUPER CREW'S SUPER SMOOTHIE

Makes 3-4 servings

Now that you have your famous smoothie store, you can make your own smoothie. The Super Crew is here to help you get started!

We've made a smoothie with ingredients from four of the Super Crew characters! Try making this smoothie and see what you think!

Ingredients:

- 1 cup frozen raspberries
- 1 cup frozen mango
- 8 oz. peach kefir milk
- 2 Tbsp. Meyer lemon juice
- ¼ cup roasted unsalted cashews
- 5 Tbsp. oats

Directions:

1. Mix the nuts and oats first, then add in the other ingredients and blend.

Tip: Kefir milk has probiotics, which are small bacteria that are good for your gut!

Can you match the Super Crew kid to the ingredient(s) that matches their powers?

MAKE YOUR OWN SMOOTHIE!

Now it's your turn to make a smoothie with at least three of the Super Crew's color power foods.

1. Choose your ingredients based on a Super Crew color food. Search through the book to discover each Super Crew kid's color powers or look at their color power circles below on both pages.
2. Then write out your ingredients and directions below so you can make the recipe again.
3. Write the name of the Super Crew kid next to each ingredient that matches their color power food.

_____'S SUPER SMOOTHIE!

(Write your name here)

Your Ingredients: **Super Crew Kid:**

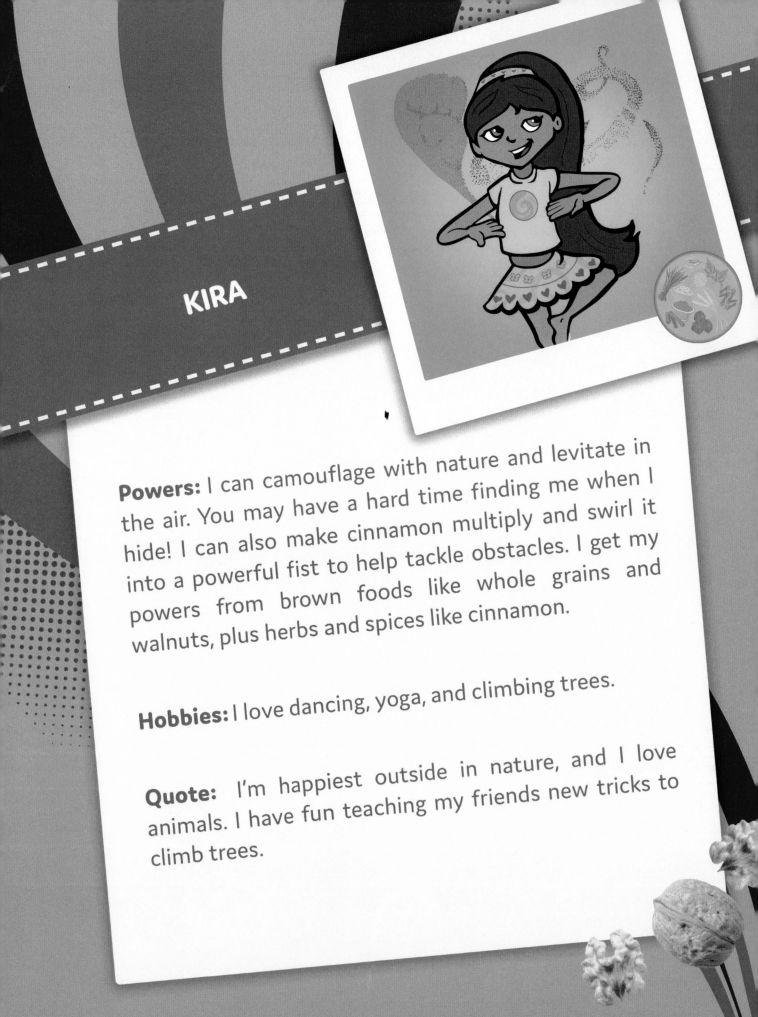

KIRA

Powers: I can camouflage with nature and levitate in the air. You may have a hard time finding me when I hide! I can also make cinnamon multiply and swirl it into a powerful fist to help tackle obstacles. I get my powers from brown foods like whole grains and walnuts, plus herbs and spices like cinnamon.

Hobbies: I love dancing, yoga, and climbing trees.

Quote: I'm happiest outside in nature, and I love animals. I have fun teaching my friends new tricks to climb trees.

EXTRA CRISPY PUMPKIN FRENCH TOAST

Makes 3-4 servings

Ingredients:

- 1 egg
- ½ cup milk
- 1 tsp. canola oil
- 1 Tbsp. honey
- 1 Tbsp. canned pumpkin (*use the rest for Andy's Pumpkin Smoothie on page 83!*)
- ½ tsp. vanilla extract
- ¼ tsp. pumpkin pie spice
- ½ tsp. cinnamon
- 1 pinch salt
- 2 tsp. healthy butter substitute
- 4-5 slices whole-grain bread

Directions:

1. Whisk egg, milk, canola oil, honey, canned pumpkin, and vanilla extract in a bowl.
2. Add in the pumpkin pie spice, cinnamon and salt into wet ingredients.
3. Place bread into egg mixture and make sure both sides are well dipped.
4. Melt 2 tsp. of butter substitute in a pan on medium-low heat.
5. Cook 1 minute on each side until light brown.
6. Dip the partly cooked toast into egg mixture again.
7. Cook for another minute on each side, until both sides are golden brown.
8. Repeat this for each slice of your whole-grain bread!

THIS RECIPE IS DELICIOUS RE-HEATED, SO MAKE EXTRA FOR A QUICK BREAKFAST DURING THE SCHOOL WEEK!

APPLE PEANUT BUTTER OATS

Makes 2 servings

Ingredients:

- ½ cup rolled oats
- 1 cup water or milk
- 2-3 Tbsp. unsweetened applesauce or grated apple
- 1 Tbsp. peanut butter or sun butter
- 1 Tbsp. ground flaxseeds or chia seeds
- 1 tsp. vanilla extract
- 1 tsp. cinnamon
- *Optional:* ½ banana for added sweetness

Directions:

1. Bring oats and water or milk to a boil. Or follow the package directions and prepare in the microwave.

2. Let simmer for about 10 minutes, stirring occasionally. In the last few minutes of cooking (once most of the liquid has been absorbed) stir in the apple, peanut butter or sun butter, ground flaxseeds, vanilla extract, and cinnamon.

Tip: *Try overnight oats to switch things up! Combine all the ingredients in a jar or glass container, mix well and store overnight in the fridge. When you wake up, enjoy cold oats ready-to-go or heat the jar for 60 seconds in the microwave.*

I love eating oatmeal in the morning because it gives me energy to be active at recess!

CHOCOLATE BREAKFAST BOWL

Makes 2-3 servings

Ingredients:

- 2 cups frozen berries like blueberries and raspberries
- 4 tsp. cocoa powder
- 2-4 tsp. chia seeds
- 10 walnuts, peanuts or unsalted nuts
- 1½-2 cups plain low-fat Greek yogurt
- Cinnamon to taste
- *Optional:* 1 tsp. honey, 1 tsp. vanilla extract

Directions:

1. Heat frozen berries in the microwave for 60-90 seconds.
2. Mix the honey, cinnamon, and vanilla extract into the warm berries.
3. Add yogurt into the bowl, then mix in cocoa.
4. Top with nuts and chia seeds.

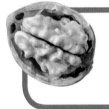

Did you ever notice how walnuts look like a brain? They're good for your brain too!

Draw your favorite breakfast in my bowl below. Add cinnamon for a sweet and healthy boost!

WHOLESOME HOMEMADE BREAD

Makes 2 loaves

Ingredients:

- 2 Tbsp. honey
- 2½ cups warm water
- 2 packages dry active yeast
- 3 cups whole-wheat flour
- 1 cup white flour + extra for cutting board
- 1 cup oat flour
- 1 cup rolled oats
- 1½ tsp. salt
- 2-3 Tbsp. olive oil, or healthy butter substitute (You may use coconut oil, however the recipe will no longer be nut-free.)

Directions:

1. Grease two bread pans generously with oil or a healthy butter substitute.

2. In a medium bowl, dissolve the honey and yeast in warm water and set aside for about 10 minutes.

3. In a large bowl, combine the dry ingredients.

4. Combine the wet ingredients with the dry, then transfer to a clean, floured surface and knead for at least 10 minutes.

5. Place dough into a lightly greased bowl, cover loosely with a clean cloth, and set aside in a warm place to let it rise for an hour.

6. Knead again for at least 10 minutes, then divide dough into two even pieces, form into the shape of loaves, place in bread pans, cover, and let it rise again for an hour.

7. Place the pans in oven and bake at 350°F for 30-40 minutes, or until the tops are golden brown.

8. Remove from the oven, transfer onto a cooling rack, and lightly oil the tops.

Tip: *This bread is delicious with honey or jam or dipped in olive oil and spices. You can slice and freeze a loaf for later - put wax paper between each slice, so it's easy to take them apart later!*

Homemade bread is fun to make on rainy days, long weekends, or chilly winter nights!

CINNAMON VANILLA MILK

Makes 2 servings

Ingredients:

- 12 oz. milk
- 1 tsp. vanilla extract
- ½ tsp. sugar
- ¼ tsp. cinnamon

Directions:

1. Mix all of the ingredients together with a spoon and enjoy!
2. If desired, heat it up on low-medium heat for a warm, comforting drink.

I ALSO LOVE KEFIR MILK BLENDED WITH A FROZEN BANANA AND CINNAMON FOR A CREAMY TASTY TREAT. THIS DRINK TASTES GREAT WITH CINNAMON RAISIN BREAD!

Cinnamon is a spice that's naturally nice! It helps keep our hearts healthy!

CINNAMON RAISIN BREAD

Makes 1 serving

Ingredients:

- 1 slice whole-grain bread
- 2 Tbsp. raisins, lightly mashed
- 1 tsp. butter or a healthy butter substitute
- Drizzle of honey
- Dash of cinnamon

Directions:

1. Toast the bread. (Use the Wholesome Home-made Bread recipe to make your own!)
2. Spread evenly with butter or healthy butter alternative.
3. Lightly mash raisins into the bread.
4. Sprinkle the bread with cinnamon, and drizzle with honey.
5. Enjoy!

YOU CAN DRESS UP WHOLE-WHEAT BREAD WITH SO MANY TASTY TOPPINGS AND SPREADS! DREAM UP SOME TASTY IDEAS TO SHARE WITH YOUR FAMILY.

It's fun to try new foods with our friends!

ACTIVITY

COLORING FUN!

"I love going to the farmers market for whole-wheat sourdough bread, figs and dates!"

ACTIVITY

WHOLE GRAIN FUN!

Directions: Help me unscramble these whole grain words! Then,
circle your favorites and underline those you will try!

conPpro

_____

rwnoB erci

_____

tmOaela

_____

rorFa

_____

uionQa

_____

layrBe

_____

tSlep

_____

hleoW-teawh

_____

What's your favorite whole grain?
How do you like to eat it?

ACTIVITY

CHECK YOUR KNOWLEDGE ON WHOLE GRAINS

Directions: Put a check next to the true statements.

- ☐ Whole grains have fiber.
- ☐ Whole grains don't provide energy.
- ☐ Whole grains have vitamins.
- ☐ Whole grains can taste good.
- ☐ Whole grains have antioxidants.
- ☐ Whole grains help you poop.
- ☐ Whole grains aren't good for your heart.

What's your favorite winter activity?
Write or draw it in the space below.

KIRA'S DRAWING ACTIVITY
Directions: Draw a whole-grain meal that you would like to eat this week, and include a fruit or vegetable!

FAVORITE WAYS TO EAT WHOLE GRAINS

Directions: Check off your favorite ways to eat whole grains.

- ☐ Whole-grain toast with peanut butter and banana slices
- ☐ Oatmeal with berries and cinnamon
- ☐ Veggie sandwich on whole-grain bread
- ☐ Whole-grain pasta with tomato and ground turkey sauce
- ☐ Brown rice with salmon and veggies

Which whole grain will you try this week?

_____

BODY POWERS!

WHOLE GRAINS GIVE YOU LONG-LASTING ENERGY AND CONTAIN F_ _ _ R & _ I _ _ _ _ _ S! THEY PROTECT YOUR _ _ A _ _!

If your best friend won't try a whole-grain food, what would you say or do to encourage them to taste it ?

SWEET SPICE & COCOA FUN!

Take Kira's taste test spice challenge!

1. Have a friend or family member make small piles of cardamom, pumpkin pie mix, ginger, and clove powders on a dish, and make an answer key of where they were placed. List the spices or herbs you're tasting on another piece of paper.

2. Close your eyes and taste one at a time. Can you guess which spice you had? On that same piece of paper, check off the spices you guessed right.

3. Underneath their names, describe how they smell and taste. Examples are hot, sweet, and/or spicy. Then, write how you would like to eat the spices with foods. Examples: pumpkin spice in overnight oats, or ginger in stir-fry.

4. Use these directions to try more spices with other friends and family members another time!

TRY ADDING NEW HERBS AND SPICES TO YOUR MEALS & SNACKS!

COCOA OR CACAO POWDER (THE RAW FORM)

Cocoa powder can be a naturally sweet addition to breakfast for a special treat. It has no added sugar, lots of fiber, and the minerals magnesium and potassium. It's good for your heart and lungs.

Circle the ways you'll try cocoa. Then write in your own tasty ideas.

- In smoothies with a frozen banana & vanilla extract
- With cinnamon and nut butter on whole-grain toast
- With heated frozen cherries
- Mixed in with almond butter

_____

_____

CAN YOU CRACK THE CODE?

Directions: I used some of my favorite foods and things in nature to create a code. Break the code to figure out my favorite spice that I enjoy like a lollipop!

CODE KEY								
N	O	C	A	S	T	I	K	M

___ ___ ___ ___ ___ ___ ___ ___

___ ___ ___ ___ ___ ___

Can you guess the name of this mystery grain?

S   **G**

_ _ _ _ _ _ _

Eating breakfast with whole grains gives me energy so I can think, focus, and do my best in school.

FOODIE ADVENTURE!

Directions: Look in this cookbook (or online) and find a cool new whole-grain recipe with one of the words from the unscramble activity. Write the recipe name below. Here are some examples: *Homemade Whole-Grain Cinnamon Raisin Bread, Oatmeal Bites, Quinoa Pilaf.*

Recipe Name: _____

Steps to making a new recipe:

1. Write down the ingredients and directions for your recipe.

2. With an adult, see which ingredients you have in your pantry or refrigerator. Make sure your ingredients aren't expired.

3. See if you have all the tools needed, like a baking dish, muffin pan, etc.

4. Check the original recipe and your list two times before heading to the store. **You don't want to forget anything!**

Whole Grain Shopping Tip: Look for the word "whole" at the beginning of the ingredients list, like whole-wheat flour, whole oats, or whole-grain brown rice. Don't be fooled by the brown color!

COLORING FUN WITH KIRA!

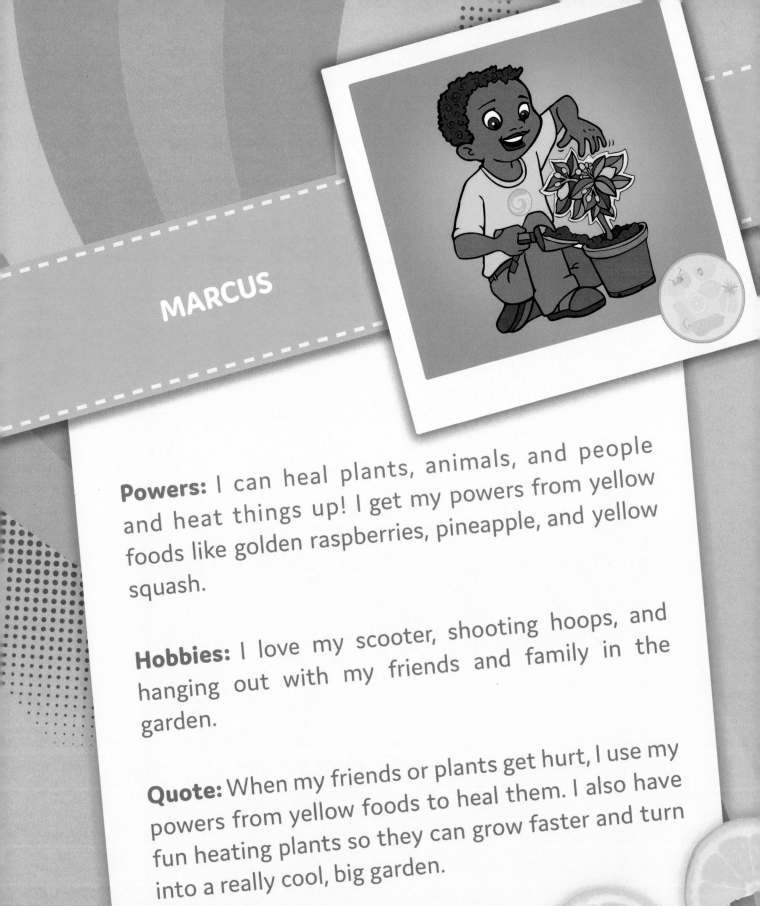

MARCUS

Powers: I can heal plants, animals, and people and heat things up! I get my powers from yellow foods like golden raspberries, pineapple, and yellow squash.

Hobbies: I love my scooter, shooting hoops, and hanging out with my friends and family in the garden.

Quote: When my friends or plants get hurt, I use my powers from yellow foods to heal them. I also have fun heating plants so they can grow faster and turn into a really cool, big garden.

PINEAPPLE CARROT MUFFINS

Makes 18 muffins

Ingredients:

- 1¼ cups all-purpose flour
- ¾ cup wheat flour
- 2 tsp. baking powder
- ½ tsp. baking soda
- ½ tsp. salt
- ½ cup + 2 tsp. vegetable oil
- ⅔-1 cup agave nectar
- 2 eggs
- 2 tsp. vanilla extract
- 2, 8-oz. cans crushed pineapple, drained well
- 2 cups carrot, shredded
- ½ cup walnuts

Directions:

1. Preheat oven to 350˚F.
2. In a large bowl combine the flours, baking powder, baking soda and salt.
3. In a separate bowl combine the oil and agave using a whisk or an electric beater.
4. Add the eggs to the oil and agave mixture and whisk to combine. Add the vanilla, pineapple, carrots and walnuts to the oil mixture and stir until combined.
5. Stir the dry ingredients into the wet ingredients and mix until just combined, making sure not to over mix.
6. Pour the batter into regular size, paper lined muffin cups.
7. Bake for 22-25 minutes, or until a toothpick comes out clean.
8. Cool for 10 minutes and enjoy!

BANANA NUT 'N' HONEY TOASTS

Makes 1-2 servings

Ingredients:

- 2 slices whole-grain bread
- 2 Tbsp. nut butter of choice (Can be made nut or peanut-free with sunflower seed butter.)
- 1 small banana
- 1 tsp. honey
- *Optional*: Cocoa powder, berries, cinnamon or vanilla extract mixed into the nut butter

Directions:

1. Toast bread to your desired crunchiness.
2. Spread nut butter, honey, and your choice of optional toppings, then enjoy!

HONEY IS MADE BY HONEY BEES FROM THE NECTAR OF FLOWERS AND PLANTS. IF HONEY IS SEALED TIGHTLY IT WON'T EXPIRE FOR DECADES! HONEY COMES IN MANY COLORS AND FLAVORS. BUY LOCAL HONEY TO SUPPORT YOUR NEIGHBORHOOD'S AGRICULTURE.

I love this banana nut toast. It's easy, tasty, sweet, and filling! I get my favorite golden honey from the farmer's market!

ACTIVITY

BEE FUN

Can you name all the parts of the bee? Use the letters in some of the boxes and the Bee Bank for a couple hints! Then give the bee a tongue by drawing it in! A bee's tongue length is very closely matched to the type of flower they pollinate. The tongue needs to be the right fit for the depth of the flower to lap up its nectar!

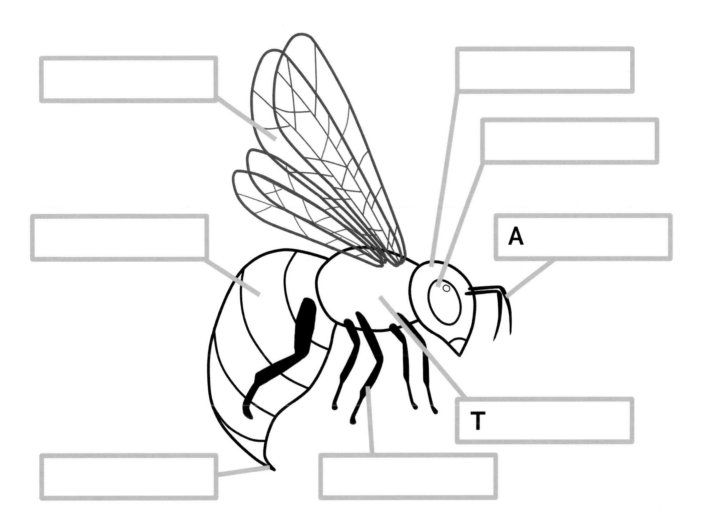

A

T

Why did the bee get married?

BEE BANK

Antennae	Abdomen
Wings	Eye
Thorax	Head
Stinger	Legs

GROW A PINEAPPLE

1. **First, pick out the perfect pineapple.** Use your senses to find the perfect one!
2. **Cut off the top.** Ask an adult to cut off the leafy top right where the flesh starts. Then remove a few of the bottom leaves.
3. **Find the baby roots.** Next, cut off the very bottom of the stem until you see brown dots on the bottom - these are where the roots will eventually grow!
4. **Let it dry out.** Turn your pineapple top upside down and allow it to dry out for about a week.
5. **Plant it!** Your pineapple top is now ready to be planted! Fill a flower pot with soil that has about 30% organic matter, such as a cactus potting mix. Plant your stem an inch deep in the soil.
6. **Water your new plant, but not too much!** Water your pineapple plant lightly, and let it dry out in between. Find a nice sunny place for it to grow.
7. **Re-pot as needed.** As your pineapple plant grows, repot it into larger containers.

Here's how to find the perfect pineapple!

Look: Look for bright green leaves and a golden brown skin. Make sure there aren't any bugs!

Feel: Your pineapple should feel firm and the scales should be securely attached.

Smell: It should smell nice and sweet!

COLORING FUN!

MARCUS' GROWING TIPS!

- Pineapple plants don't like freezing temperatures - bring yours inside in the winter if the temperatures drop where you live.
- Your pineapple will grow but it may take up to three years for your plant to grow fruit, so be patient! Look for blossoms, which will eventually turn into new pineapple fruit! YUM!

PLAYING DETECTIVE!

Can you help me uncover the following words that begin with
the letter Y? Use the word bank below if needed.

The day before today.

— — — — — — — — —

Tapioca is made from this root veggie.

— — — — —

A stretchy form of exercise.

— — — —

A place near home with grass where kids play.

— — — —

Check off which tasty pineapple treats you'll try.

☐ Add pineapple to a blender with banana, yogurt, and ice (or any of your favorite fruit) for a sweet smoothie!

☐ Slice up a pineapple, cool it in the fridge, and enjoy it on a hot summer day!

☐ Add pineapple chunks to cottage cheese for a light lunch or tasty afternoon snack!

☐ Your own sensational snack:

_____

LET'S PLAY A GAME!

Two players take turns drawing line segments between each yellow dot in their own color pen. The object is to draw a square without drawing over your own line.
Hint: There will only be one winner!

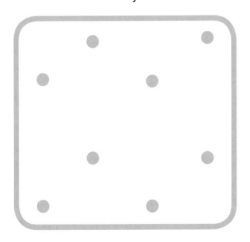

Pineapples are a yellow colored tropical fruit that are loaded with nutrients.

Word Bank: yucca, yard, yesterday, yoga

NUTTY CARROT FUN!

The farmers market is a fun way to see all different colors of fruits and veggies!
Carrots come in **purple**, yellow, **white** and orange. Color them in below.

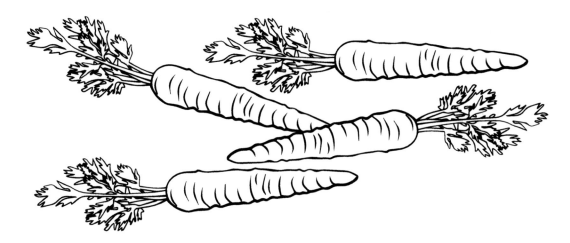

Try these great carrot combinations:

☐ Yellow carrots or bananas with peanut butter

☐ Orange carrots with hummus

☐ Purple or white carrots minced and sautéed then added to omelets

☐ Shredded in breakfast muffins - see page 31

What's your favorite way to eat nut butter or sun butter? Write it here.

Draw a funny face and hair on the banana.

START-STOP-KEEP WITH THE SUPER CREW

Think about all the tasty food and fun activities you've learned about. Now play a game with the Super Crew and your family called Start-Stop-Keep! Name one thing you will start today, one you will stop today, and one healthy thing you will keep doing!

the **SUPER CREW**

START
Example: Replace refined flours at breakfast with tasty whole grains like whole-wheat French toast or overnight oats.

Your turn: _____

_____

STOP
Example: Watching TV too much.

Your turn: _____

_____

KEEP
Example: Eating fruit with breakfast.

Your turn: _____

_____

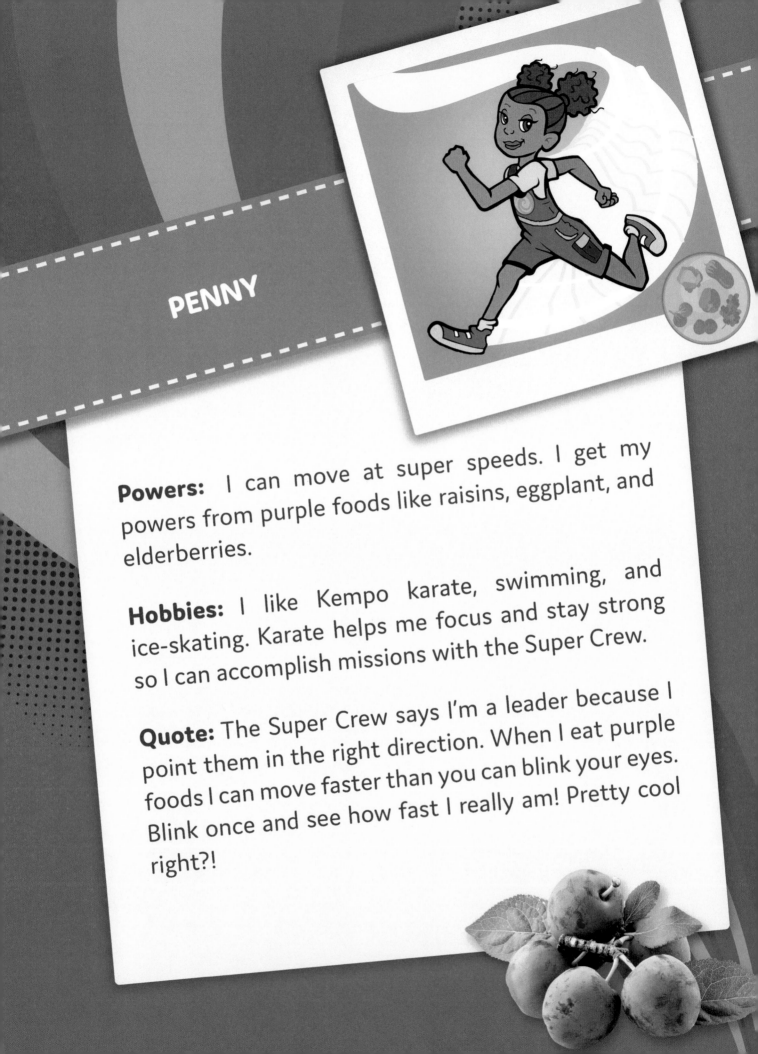

PENNY

Powers: I can move at super speeds. I get my powers from purple foods like raisins, eggplant, and elderberries.

Hobbies: I like Kempo karate, swimming, and ice-skating. Karate helps me focus and stay strong so I can accomplish missions with the Super Crew.

Quote: The Super Crew says I'm a leader because I point them in the right direction. When I eat purple foods I can move faster than you can blink your eyes. Blink once and see how fast I really am! Pretty cool right?!

ACAI, CHIA AND DRIED PLUM BOWL

Makes 1-2 servings

Ingredients:

- ½ cup frozen spinach
- 1 sweetened frozen acai smoothie packet (commonly available at big grocery chains)
- 1 cup frozen blueberries
- ½ cup frozen mango
- 3 Tbsp. Meyer lemon juice
- 1 cup milk (we used unsweetened soy milk)

Toppings:

- A few banana slices
- 1 tsp. chia seeds
- A few bits of dark chocolate

Directions:

1. Measure all of the ingredients and place in blender.
2. Blend, periodically pausing to mix ingredients with a spoon.
3. Serve in a bowl and add toppings.
4. Enjoy!

PURPLE FOODS ARE GOOD FOR YOUR HEART.

BLACKBERRY CHIA PUDDING

Makes 3-4 servings

Ingredients:

- 1 cup milk
- 1, 5.6-oz. container of flavored Greek yogurt (we used mango)
- 4 Tbsp. nonfat plain Greek yogurt
- 2 tsp. Maple syrup
- 1 tsp. vanilla extract
- ½ tsp. lemon zest
- ¼ cup chia seeds
- 1 cup blackberries (fresh or frozen)

Directions:

1. Whisk milk, yogurt, maple syrup, vanilla extract, and lemon zest together.
2. Add in chia seeds and whisk well again.
3. Cover tightly and place in the refrigerator.
4. Add in blackberries in the morning and serve.

I LIKE TO FREEZE PURPLE GRAPES AND ADD THEM TO MY BREAKFAST YOGURT, CHIA PUDDING OR SMOOTHIES. THEY MAKE BREAKFAST SWEET AND FLAVORFUL!

Sometimes I use pomegranate or passion fruit yogurt. I like to add orange zest too!

WHAT DO YOU BEE-LIEVE?

Penny knows bees are in peril because of poor nutrition, pesticides, and parasites. She cares about bees because they help pollinate her favorite foods!

Check off each new fact you learn as you read it:

☐ Bees are the reason we get to enjoy so many fruits and vegetables!

☐ Flowering plants produce pollen that is picked up by bees.

☐ The bees transfer this pollen to other plants so they can produce a flower, fruit, or vegetable.

☐ Honey bees communicate with each other by dancing.

I love the queen bee *bee*cause I'm a natural leader too!

Which honey bee facts do you think are true? Write T for true next to any fact about honey bees. Ask your parents for help.

_____ 1. Bees are insects that have six legs.

_____ 2. Bees only have a single eye.

_____ 3. Bees eat and drink pollen.

_____ 4. Bees talk to each other by dancing.

_____ 5. All types of bees make honey.

_____ 6. Bees are the only insect to make food for humans.

_____ 7. Worker honey bees are all females.

PENNY'S DRAWING ACTIVITY

Directions: In the box below, draw your favorite food that comes from a plant. Next to it, write a little thank you to the bees for helping it pollinate!

PURPLE FOODS

Why does Penny like purple grapes? Purple grapes are full of a group of fight-o-nutrients that help keep us healthy. Find out what this group is called with the clue in this bunch of grapes!

A   N   T   I   O   _   _   _   _   _   _   _

Being active every day is good for my heart too!

Can you say **Penny purchased purple potatoes**, five times fast?

DISCOVER PURPLE FOODS WITH PENNY!

Blackberries can look purple too! They have anthocyanins – a plant fight-o-nutrient that's good for the heart.

Other purple foods:

• Red cabbage – looks purple
• Purple potatoes – are purple inside and out!
• Eggplant – has purple skin
• Blueberries – some varieties are more purple than blue
• Plums – are fiber-rich dark purple treats

Can you name any other purple foods? Write them below.

ACTIVITY

GUESS WHAT'S DIFFERENT

Directions: Penny ran so fast that some things in the picture moved or fell off the page. Compare each picture then circle the differences in the bottom image.

Hint: There are at least 10 differences.

THE SUPER CREW'S BERRY BREAKFAST PARFAIT

Makes 2 parfaits

Ingredients:

- ⅔ cup oats
- 2 tsp. vegetable oil
- 1 tsp. honey
- 3 Tbsp. walnut pieces
- 1 tsp. cinnamon
- 1-2 Tbsp. ground flaxseeds
- 1 cup fresh or frozen berries
- 1½ cups plain nonfat or low-fat yogurt

Directions:

1. Combine oats, oil, honey, walnuts, and cinnamon and mix well. You can use this mixture as-is in your parfait.

2. For extra crunch, place in a toaster oven or broiler for about 5 minutes.

3. In a bowl, jar, or wide-mouthed glass, place alternating layers of yogurt, berries, oats, and flaxseed.

4. Enjoy!

As they would say in France, this berry breakfast parfait really is 'parfait' (perfect)!

Eating a healthy breakfast helps us think and feel our best!

SUPER BABY ABIGAIL'S PARFAIT FUN!

Pretend you're making the most famous and fancy parfait of all time! What makes it so special? Is it topped with edible flowers? Draw what makes it so tasty and unique. List the ingredients below.

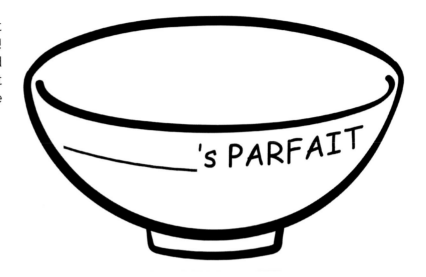

Describe the flavors and textures in your parfait. Examples: sweet, creamy, crunchy, etc.

CHEF _____'S FABULOUS PARFAIT

(Write your name here)

Write your ingredients below with a crayon or colored pencil that matches the color of the food. Then circle the plant-based ingredients.

"What's a vampire's favorite fruit?"

Hint: *It's a type of citrus*

THE SUPER CREW'S FRUIT SUSHI

Makes 2 servings

This is a fun way to get creative at breakfast. Try the Super Crew's twist on sushi!

Ingredients:

- 1 large whole-wheat or whole-grain tortilla
- 3 Tbsp. flavored Greek yogurt or plain yogurt with 1 tsp. honey
- 2-3 strawberries, sliced
- 1 fresh peach or nectarine, chopped
- 1 kiwi, sliced thinly
- *Optional:* Sprinkle of cinnamon

Directions:

1. First, lay the tortilla flat on a plate or clean countertop.
2. If using plain yogurt, mix in the honey with a spoon until smooth.
3. If you want to use cinnamon, add it to the yogurt mixture.
4. Spread the yogurt mixture across the tortilla with a spoon.
5. Layer the fruit across the tortilla.
6. Roll the tortilla long ways and slice into "sushi" roll pieces.
7. For fun, try eating with chopsticks!

Strawberries give me extra water powers because they naturally contain water!

Whole-wheat flour tortillas are my favorite!

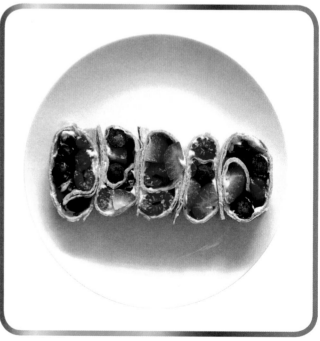

THE SUPER CREW'S BREAKFAST PIZZA

Makes 1-2 servings

Ingredients:

- 1 whole-wheat English muffin or GF brown rice tortilla
- 3 Tbsp. tomato sauce
- ⅛-¼ cup shredded mozzarella cheese or vegan cheese
- ¼ tsp. dried basil or oregano
- *Optional:* 1 tsp. fresh basil

Directions:

1. Toast the English muffin or tortilla.
2. Lightly cover the muffin or tortilla with tomato sauce.
3. Evenly sprinkle cheese, oregano, and basil on top.
4. Place in the toaster at 350°F for 5 minutes until the cheese is evenly melted!
5. It's pizza time!

BASIL IS LOADED WITH ANTIOXIDANTS. TWO TABLESPOONS OF DRIED BASIL HAS TWO TIMES AS MANY ANTIOXIDANTS AS A CUP OF GREEN GRAPES.

Breakfast can be any healthy meal. It doesn't have to be a popular breakfast food to start your day!

Adding fresh or dried herbs makes it taste even better!

TOM-TOM

Powers: I can move and shape water. I get my powers from red foods like tomatoes, watermelon, and radish. Plus, drinking water gives me superpowers too!

Hobbies: I like to play around water and make tidal waves, especially on hot days when I need to cool down from the sun!

Quote: I can get a little feisty around water, at least that's what my big sis Jessie says. I can't help that when I giggle, I make bubbles big enough to float in!

HEARTY APPLESAUCE

Makes 6 servings

Ingredients:

- 6 apples (of your choice!), cored and sliced
- 2 tsp. cinnamon

Directions:

1. Bring enough water to a boil to fill underneath a steam basket.
2. Place the steam basket in the pot with the apples on top. Steam apples with the lid on the pot for 10-12 minutes.
3. When the apples are tender and a fork passes through them easily, place the apples in a blender with the cinnamon and blend together.
4. Enjoy some now and keep the rest in a jar in the fridge for another time!

WHEN BAKING, USE APPLESAUCE TO CUT DOWN ON SUGAR AND OIL IN A RECIPE. IT WILL ADD MOISTURE AND SWEETNESS, PLUS SOME FIGHT-O-NUTRIENT POWER!

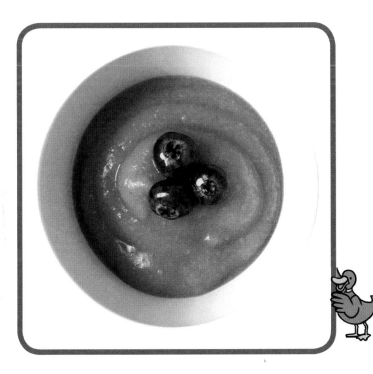

STRAWBERRY OAT SCONES

Makes 8 scones

Ingredients:

- 1 cup oat flour (you can make your own by grinding rolled oats in food processor or blender)
- ½ cup cornmeal, finely ground (you can grind with your oat flour)
- 1 cup whole-wheat flour
- 2 tsp. cinnamon
- 1½ tsp. baking powder
- ¼ tsp. salt
- ¼ cup coconut flakes
- ½ cup honey
- 1 egg
- 1 cup sliced strawberries (either fresh or frozen)
- 4 Tbsp. Greek yogurt
- ¼ cup canola oil
- *Optional:* ½ cup dark chocolate chips

Directions:

1. Preheat oven to 375°F.
2. In two different bowls, mix dry and wet ingredients separately.
3. Add the wet ingredients into the dry and mix until just combined.
4. Mold into your favorite scone shape and place on a lightly oiled cookie sheet.
5. Bake for 20-25 minutes, or until fully cooked through. Then, remove from the oven and let cool.

EAT YOUR WATER

Did you know that some foods are more than 90% water? There are a lot of fruits and veggies of all different colors that are filled with water!

Directions: Circle the foods that are red, which is Tom-Tom's favorite color! Then underline the foods you will try or already enjoy. Finally, guess which 5 foods have the highest amount of water and a put a star next to them.

_____ Strawberries   _____ Cucumbers

_____ Grapefruit   _____ Radishes

_____ Lettuce   _____ Watermelon

_____ Jicama (hik-ah-ma)   _____ Tomatoes

Directions: There are 16 ounces in this glass measuring cup. How many tablespoons are there? _____

Use the key to figure it out. Then cut up 3 cups of watermelon and blend it. How many cups are there now? _____

Guide for liquid measurements:

2 tablespoons = 1 ounce

4 tablespoons = 2 ounces

8 ounces = 1 cup

16 ounces = 2 cups

8 ounces = _____ tablespoons

16 ounces = _____ tablespoons

Directions: If you could rename the foods above, what would call them? Come up with their new names below then write or draw a couple ways to eat them.
Examples: Strawberries – sweet triangles, Jicama (hik-ah-ma) – Mexican potato.

WATER FUN

Fun in the Sun!

What do you like to do in the pool or at the waterpark? Write two ideas of your own, then check off your two favorites from the list below.

- ☐ See how many laps you can swim
- ☐ Listen to music
- ☐ Go on water slides
- ☐ Use a kick board
- ☐ Play water volleyball with friends
- ☐ _____
- ☐ _____

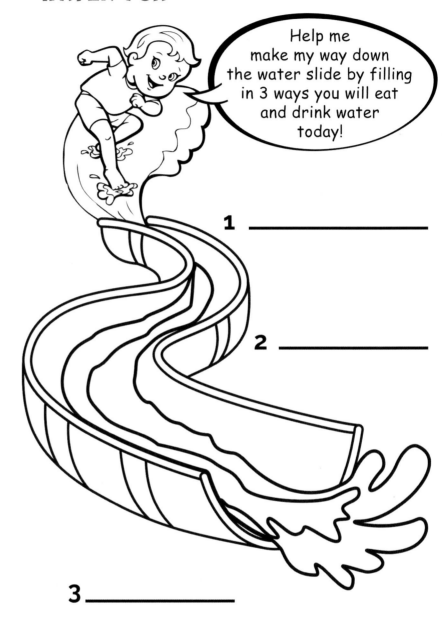

Help me make my way down the water slide by filling in 3 ways you will eat and drink water today!

1 _____

2 _____

3 _____

Our bodies need water every day to stay healthy and hydrated!

How will you hydrate? Check off what you'll try:

- ☐ I'll add fruit or veggie slices to my water.
- ☑ I'll get a reusable water bottle and make it my new best friend, taking it with me wherever I go to stay hydrated all day!

What is one fruit you want to try in your water bottle?
Write the name of it, then draw it below and color it in!

ACTIVITY

WORD PLAY AND CONNECT THE DOTS

Connect the dots to reveal the fruit. Next, color this fruit.
Hint: This fruit comes in more than one color!

Tom-Tom's tasty applesauce can be mixed into other foods to make them naturally sweet, or it can be a tasty side dish. How do you want to eat your applesauce?

_____

_____

_____

_____

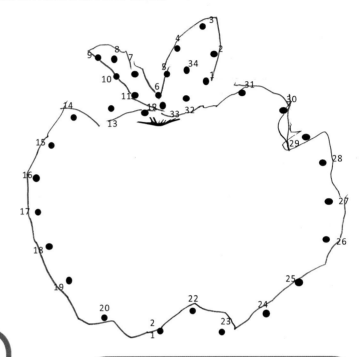

WORD PLAY

Kira loves cinnamon the spice and the Super Crew's dog! What words can you make from **Cinnamon**? Play with these 8 letters to make new words and list them below. Use another piece of paper to list more! There are over 20 words.

Example: coin

_____

_____

_____

What's your favorite red fruit, vegetable or spice? Draw it in the box below.

53

THE SUPER CREW'S BROWN RICE CAKES 4 TASTY WAYS!

Each combination makes 1 serving

Brown rice cakes are a crunchy whole grain way to start the day. They also boost fiber and variety! They come in circle or square shapes. Mix the ingredients together, except the fruit or veggies which are placed on top. Spread the ingredients below on top of a rice cake and enjoy.

Fig & Raspberry:

• 1 brown rice cracker
• 4 Tbsp. ricotta cheese
• 2-3 tsp. raspberry jam
• ½ tsp. cocoa
• 4 chopped dried figs

Hummus & Cucumber:

• 1 brown rice cracker
• 2 Tbsp. hummus
• ⅛ cup chopped cucumber
• ⅛ tsp. cumin

Dreamy Raspberry Cocoa Bliss:

• 1 brown rice cracker
• 1 Tbsp. tahini
• ½ tsp. cocoa powder
• 5-10 raspberries
• Some bits of broken chocolate pieces

Banana, Nut & Honey:

• 1 brown rice cracker
• 1½ Tbsp. nut butter or sun butter
• ½ banana, sliced
• ½ tsp. honey drizzled
• Sprinkle of cinnamon

I love healthy crunchy whole grains.

THE SUPER CREW'S SALTY, SWEET & SAVORY BREAKFAST

Makes 1 serving

Baby sweet peppers are so sweet and taste great any time of day. Roast them with olive oil, then add them to breakfast dishes (omelets, burritos), lunch wraps, or eat as a side at dinner.

Ingredients:

- ½ whole-wheat English muffin
- ¼ cup roasted red and yellow sweet peppers
- ¼ cup Kalamata olives
- ¼ tsp. olive oil

Directions:

1. Wash and slice peppers.
2. Lightly coat pan and peppers with olive oil. Cook at 400°F for 10 minutes or until soft.
3. Toast the English muffin.
4. Chop the olives and peppers into small pieces and mix them together in a small bowl with the olive oil. Or use food processor to blend.
5. Put your olive, pepper, and oil mixture on top of your toasted muffin.
6. Enjoy!

I love sweet red baby peppers as a snack – either crunchy or cooked with olive oil.

Sometimes I'm in the mood for a savory breakfast with a touch of sweetness! I love making this with my dad!

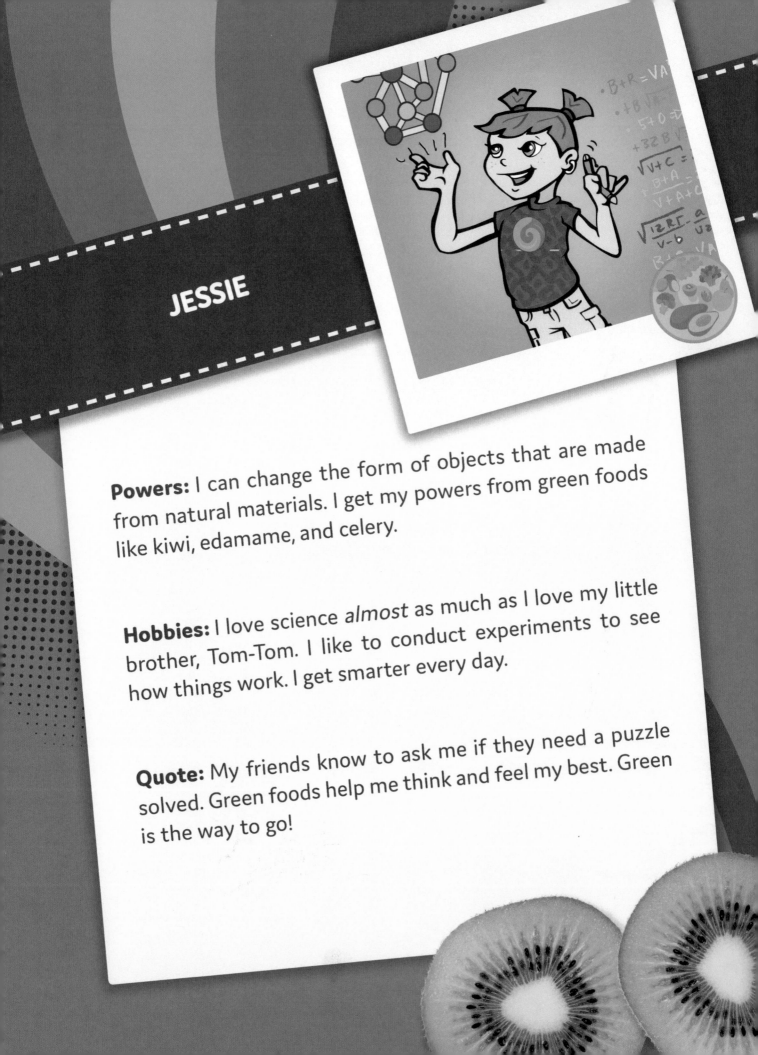

JESSIE

Powers: I can change the form of objects that are made from natural materials. I get my powers from green foods like kiwi, edamame, and celery.

Hobbies: I love science *almost* as much as I love my little brother, Tom-Tom. I like to conduct experiments to see how things work. I get smarter every day.

Quote: My friends know to ask me if they need a puzzle solved. Green foods help me think and feel my best. Green is the way to go!

FRUIT AND YOGURT GREEN SMOOTHIE

Makes 1-2 servings

Ingredients:

- 1 banana
- ¾ cup berries (blueberries, raspberries, or other berries)
- ½ cup plain nonfat yogurt
- ½ cup baby spinach
- 1 Tbsp. almond butter or other nut butter
- ¼ cup water
- 1 tsp. honey

Directions:

1. Add all ingredients to the blender.
2. Blend together until smooth.
3. Serve and enjoy!

 **KIWIS, GRAPES, AND CURLY KALE ARE GOOD IN SMOOTHIES. PARSLEY WITH APPLES AND PINEAPPLE IS TASTY TOO.**

Have fun blending and whirling these ingredients together for a tasty and colorful smoothie!

VEGGIE BREAKFAST BURRITO

Makes 1 serving

Tip: Double or triple the recipe to make some to share!

Ingredients:

- ¼ russet potato
- 2-3 cremini mushrooms, well cleaned
- ⅓ zucchini or patty pan squash
- 2 kale leaves
- 2 tsp. olive oil
- 1 egg
- ¼ cup shredded cheddar cheese
- 1-2 Tbsp. salsa (choose low-sodium when possible)
- 1 whole-grain tortilla
- *Optional:* ¼ cup pinto or black beans, avocado

Directions:

1. Dice the potato and cook in a skillet over medium heat.
2. Add ¼ cup water and cover with a lid to speed up the cooking process.
3. While the potato is cooking, dice the zucchini and mushrooms. Add these to the skillet when the potato is almost fully cooked, along with the olive oil.
4. Rip the kale into small pieces and mix the egg, then add these to the skillet. If adding beans, drain, rinse, and add to the skillet as well. Let cook until the egg is fully cooked through and the kale is tender.
5. Warm the tortilla, then transfer the skillet mixture and the remaining ingredients to the tortilla. Roll it all up into a burrito and enjoy as a balanced breakfast.

The green foods in my breakfast burrito protect my body!

RECIPE

HERBY EGG WHITES

Makes 1 serving

Ingredients:

- 2 egg whites
- 1 tsp. olive oil
- ⅛ tsp. dried oregano
- ⅛ tsp. dried basil
- ⅛ tsp. onion salt
- ¼ tsp. Trader Joes' 21 Seasoning Salute or your favorite Mrs. Dash Herb & Spice mix

Directions:

1. Drizzle the olive oil in a nonstick pan and grease the entire pan, including the edges, with your fingers or a silicon spatula.
2. Crack the eggs and separate out the whites from yolk and throw out the yolk or use for baking. Pour the egg whites into a non-heated pan and spread out across the pan.
3. Heat the pan on medium heat.
4. While the egg becomes more translucent white, evenly sprinkle in the seasonings.
5. Use a spatula to fold the egg mixture until it's log-shaped.
6. Use a pizza roller or knife to cut.
7. Enjoy on its own or with whole-grain bread, fruit or avocado.

Eggs taste so delicious with fresh or dried herbs. This is one of my favorite combos!

HIGH PROTEIN PEAR PANCAKES

Makes 8 servings of medium size pancakes

Make a big batch of these and freeze some of them so you can enjoy them later! To freeze, separate each pancake with a 2-inch square of wax paper, then seal in airtight packaging. You can defrost a few in the fridge the night before. Warm them up with nut butter or butter and syrup or grab them and eat them cold for breakfast on the go!

Ingredients:

- 2 cups oat flour (blend your own oats to make oat flour)
- 4 tsp. baking powder
- ¼ tsp. salt
- ⅓ tsp. cinnamon
- Smidgeon of nutmeg
- 2 eggs
- 4 halves canned pears, mashed
- ½ cup cottage cheese
- ½ cup milk or milk substitute
- ¼ cup canola oil
- 1 tsp. vanilla extract

Directions:

1. Combine the flour, baking powder, cinnamon, salt, and nutmeg in a large bowl and stir together.

2. In a separate bowl, mash the pears with a fork to create small lumps and chunks.

3. Add the cottage cheese, eggs, milk or milk substitute, oil, and vanilla, and stir well to combine.

4. Add the wet ingredients to the bowl containing the flour mixture and whisk well to fully incorporate the ingredients.

5. To prepare the pancakes, lightly oil a griddle, cast iron, or other heavy-bottomed pan and heat over medium-high heat.

6. Reduce the heat to medium-low, add about ⅓ cup of batter per pancake, and cook until bubbles form over the surface of the batter.

7. Flip the pancake and cook 30 seconds to 1 minute on the other side, or until both sides of the pancake are dark golden brown.

ZUCCHINI MUFFINS

Makes 12-14 muffins

Ingredients:

- 1 cup whole-wheat flour
- ¾ cup oat flour (or blend whole oats to make your own flour)
- ½ cup brown sugar, lightly packed
- 1 tsp. cinnamon
- 1¼ tsp. baking powder
- ½ tsp. baking soda
- ¼ tsp. salt
- 1⅓ cups shredded zucchini (press out extra liquid)
- ½ cup milk or milk alternative
- 2 large eggs
- 4 Tbsp. canola oil

Directions:

1. Preheat oven to 400°F and lightly grease muffin tin with oil.
2. If you're making your own oat flour, blend oats in food processor until they're a fine consistency, then place in a large mixing bowl.
3. Mix all dry ingredients into a large mixing bowl.
4. Wash zucchini and shred by hand or in a food processor, press out extra liquid, and place in a second large mixing bowl.
5. Add milk, eggs, and oil to zucchini bowl.
6. Create a well in the middle of the dry ingredients and add wet ingredients. Mix briefly.
7. Fill muffin tins to about ¾ full.
8. Bake at 400°F for 15-20 minutes or until a toothpick inserted into the center comes out clean.
9. Let cool and enjoy!

HERBY APPLE SAUSAGE

Makes 8 servings

Ingredients:

- 1 lb. ground turkey
- ½ tsp. black pepper
- 1 Tbsp. fresh sage
- 1 Tbsp. fresh thyme
- ½ Tbsp. fresh rosemary
- ¼ tsp. smoked paprika
- ⅛ tsp. cayenne
- ¼ tsp. cumin
- ⅛ tsp. onion powder
- ¼ tsp. garlic powder
- 5 grinds fresh ground pepper
- ¼ tsp. salt
- 1 Tbsp. canola or olive oil
- ¼ cup chopped apple, microwaved

Directions:

1. Wash your hands with warm water and soap before you begin and also after you finish handling the raw turkey.
2. Wash, chop then bake apple in microwave for 90 seconds. Let apple cool.
3. Wash and mince all herbs.
4. Coat a large skillet with cooking spray or coat with oil.
5. Mix all ingredients together in a bowl very thoroughly using your hands if necessary.
6. Make the mixture into 1-2 inch balls and flatten on the skillet.
7. Place skillet on medium-high heat.
8. Cook each patty 3 minutes on each side until they're no longer pink inside and the internal temperature is at 165˚F. Do not overcook, or they will be dry.
9. Once cooled using wax paper, separate each patty and freeze in an airtight container.
10. Serve with eggs and whole-wheat toast or a fruit smoothie.

We grow herbs on the front porch in a pot. Tom-Tom helped plant the seedlings and I water them before school.

I like these sausages with whole grain pancakes on weekends.

FRIED RICE WITH EGG AND PEAS

Makes 4 servings

Ingredients:

- 3 cups cooked brown rice
- 2 eggs
- 1 cup frozen green peas
- 3 Tbsp. olive oil
- 2 Tbsp. Bragg Liquid Aminos (or low-sodium soy sauce)
- ¼ tsp. garlic powder

Directions:

1. This recipe is perfect with left-over rice, or you can cook a new batch!
2. Heat a medium-sized pan on medium-low heat and add 1 Tbsp. of olive oil and crack two eggs directly into the pan.
3. Stir vigorously using a small spatula to scramble the eggs until they are cooked into small pieces.
4. Add 3 cups of cooked brown rice and 1 cup of frozen green peas into the pan and add the remaining 2 Tbsp. of olive oil.
5. Maintain heat and fold in rice, peas and eggs. Mix well for 2½ minutes.
6. Increase heat to medium and add 2 Tbsp. of Bragg Liquid Aminos and ¼ tsp. of garlic powder.
7. Turn the rice mixture over multiple times until the Bragg Liquid Aminos and garlic powder are combined evenly.
8. Serve immediately and enjoy!

Eating a healthy breakfast helps me think my best at school!

CREAMY DREAMY SMOOTHIE & SMOOTHIE BOWL

Makes 2 servings

Recipe 1 Ingredients:

- 1 ripe green pear with skin
- 2 golden kiwis
- 1 cup frozen mango
- ¼ cup frozen spinach
- 1 cup OJ
- ⅛ cup roasted unsalted cashews (add more for a creamier texture)
- 8-10 ice cubes

Recipe 2 Ingredients:

- Leftover serving from Recipe 1
- ⅓ cup Cheerios
- 5 roasted unsalted cashews
- 3-5 ice cubes

Recipe 1 Directions:

1. Combine all ingredients except the ice and mix well.
2. Once fully blended, add 8-10 ice cubes and blend well.
3. If you make extra, place the blender back in the refrigerator for tomorrow.

Recipe 2 Directions:

1. Add ice to the leftover smoothie and blend again.
2. Pour in a bowl and top with whole-grain cereal. Choose one with less than 6 grams of sugar per serving!
3. Add in roasted unsalted cashews.

TOT VEGGIE SCRAMBLE

Makes 2-4 servings

Ingredients:

- 3 eggs
- 2 Tbsp. shredded cheddar cheese
- ½ cup broccoli florets, chopped into baby bite size pieces
- ¼ red onion, diced
- 1-3 tsp. avocado oil or olive oil per your preference
- Pinch of salt
- Pinch of pepper

Directions:

1. In a small bowl whisk together the eggs, salt, and pepper and set aside.
2. Heat a medium skillet over medium heat.
3. Add the avocado oil to the skillet.
4. Sauté the onions and broccoli over medium heat until the onions are clear - about 5 minutes.
5. Add the eggs to the veggies and cook until eggs are cooked through - about another 5 minutes.
6. Top with shredded cheese.
7. Serve with some fresh fruit like berries!

HOMEMADE DINOSAUR CEREAL BITES

Makes 4-6 servings

Jessie made these for Tom-Tom when he had his first foods. Try these with your younger child!

Ingredients:

- ½ cup Tom-Tom's Hearty Applesauce recipe on page 49
- ¾ cup oat flour
- 1 Tbsp. olive oil
- 2 eggs
- 1 tsp. baking powder
- 1 cup spinach

Directions:

1. Preheat oven to 350°F.
2. Combine the ingredients in a blender or food processor.
3. Place mixture in a pastry bag or plastic bag with the tip cut off.
4. On a baking sheet lined with wax paper, put batter down in small ¼-inch circles.
5. Bake in oven at 350°F for 10 minutes, and then reduce heat to 250°F and bake an additional 40 minutes.

AVOCADO TOAST 3 WAYS

Makes 1-2 servings

Ingredients:

- 1 small avocado
- ⅛ tsp. cumin
- ⅛ tsp. smoked paprika
- ⅛ tsp. salt
- 1 tsp. lime juice
- 1 slice whole-wheat toast or gluten-free tortilla
- 1 egg (hardboiled or fried) *or* 2 oz. smoked salmon

Directions:

1. Choose which variation you want to make.
   a. To hard-boil eggs, place eggs in a large pot and cover with 1 inch of cool water. Bring water to rolling boil for 2 minutes then turn off heat and cover for 10-12 minutes. Cool in ice water, then store in the refrigerator.
   b. To fry the eggs, heat oil on medium-high heat, then cook egg until it's cooked through.
   c. If you are using the smoked salmon, cut into four even pieces.
2. Mash 1 small avocado with ⅛ tsp. cumin, ⅛ tsp. smoked paprika, ⅛ tsp salt, and 1 tsp. lime juice.
3. Mash and mix together in a bowl.
4. Toast bread for a crunchier taste.
5. Spread avocado mixture on the whole-wheat toast or GF tortilla.
6. Spread out hardboiled egg or place fried egg or smoked salmon on top!

> I love making avocado toast with all different toppings! Here are 3 of my favorites. Circle which one you'll try first!

MAKING SMOOTHIE BOWLS

Smoothie bowls are simply thicker smoothies that are eaten with a spoon. Use less liquid and add chia seeds, nut butters, or avocados to make them thicker.

Did you know that you can make any smoothie into a smoothie bowl? Draw the recipe ingredients you want to use. Look through the book for topping ideas.

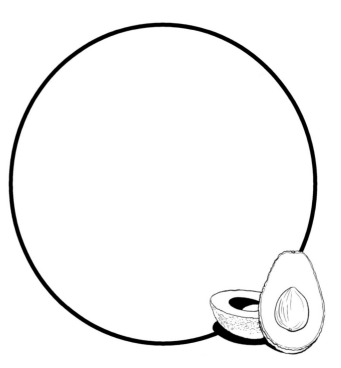

List your ingredients:

_____

_____

_____

_____

_____

Make the lemon into a funny face!

Check off the ingredients you think will taste good in your smoothie bowl:

- ☐ Blended avocado
- ☐ A little bit of Meyer lemon juice
- ☐ Frozen fruit
- ☐ Chia seeds or nuts

ACTIVITY

EGGY FACTS

Egg shells come in many different colors based on the type of chicken laying the egg. Look up the different colors, and color in your half-dozen pack with the different ones you find!

What healthy plant-based foods will you serve with your different styles of eggs? Check them off:

☐ Hard boiled on whole-grain toast

☐ Fried on top of oatmeal

☐ Scrambled with herbs and spices

☐ In a breakfast burrito with sweet or spicy peppers

Eggs taste great with many different types of herbs. Circle the herbs in the list to the right that you've tried before and underline the herbs you want to try next.

sage
rosemary
chives
thyme
cilantro
parsley

Herbs are loaded with antioxidants and give my meals a flavor boost. Try freezing your extra herbs. Next time you make your favorite meals with herbs, you'll have them ready to go!

MATH RIDDLES

Jessie has shared 4 of her favorite green foods. Match the number to the correct letter to solve the riddles. The secret word is what's at the center of one of her favorite green fruits.

YOUR GUIDE:

A	B	C	D	E	F	G	H	I	J	K	L	M
24	15	1	12	4	19	2	13	23	9	3	20	7

N	O	P	Q	R	S	T	U	V	W	X	Y	Z
25	~~14~~	5	21	11	18	6	22	17	8	16	10	26

I love science and equations. Number and letter scrambles are my favorite!

YOUR TURN:

24	17	14	1	24	12	14

15	11	**14**	1	1	14	20	23

1	23	20	24	25	6	**11**	14

2	11	24	5	**4**	18

Can you find the secret word made with the bolded numbers?

—— —— —— ——

Calculate the secret number made with the bolded numbers?

___ + ___ + ___ + ___ = (___)

Hint to secret number: If you tried a new food each day in the month of June, how many new foods would you have tried?

LEAFY GREENS

Jessie loves adding dark leafy greens to her meals because green foods
are good for your whole body! She really likes curly kale.

Directions: Check one or more of the green foods below you'll try this week. Then underline
the leafy green you think will taste best in a smoothie. What else is in your smoothie?
Write the foods you're adding in your smoothie next to the cup, then color it in.

☐   **Collard greens:** very popular in the south

☐   **Swiss chard:** fun and easy to grow in a pot

☐   **Kale:** tasty blended in smoothie bowls or as chips with chili powder and salt

☐   **Spinach:** yummy in a breakfast omelet

Foods in your smoothie:

Breakfast
omelets are often made
with cooked veggies. Some
restaurants serve omelets with
a side of leafy greens or
avocado. What veggie will
you try in your
omelet?

_____'s
Smoothie

GREEN FOOD GUESSING GAME

Guess which foods are below based on the descriptions. Color them based on your color and taste preferences. Jessie likes all color plant-based foods even though green is her favorite! **Hint:** They are in the ingredient list of Jessie's green smoothie on page 64!

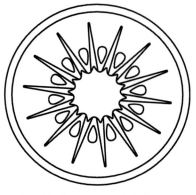

I have yellow or green skin. I am watery and crunchy.

My skin is brown. My heart can be green or golden.

I can be white, light yellow or ivory. I am very hard.

I AM A

I AM A

I AM A

_____.

_____.

_____.

How would you draw the above ingredients differently?

GROWING PEAS WITH JESSIE

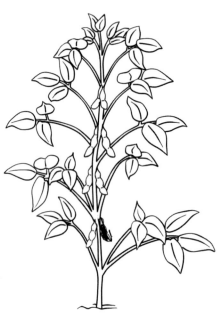

Green peas grow in pods on a plant. To find the peas, you have to crack the pod open and pop them out. How many pods can you find on this bush? Color them in, then color the rest of your plant! Peas can be green or purple!

Number of pods: _____

FOOD GROUPS AND YOUR MENU

Here is this week's menu for Tom-Tom and me. I like having a menu to make morning time easier.

BREAKFAST	DAY
Avocado Toast	Monday + Tuesday
Fruit and Yogurt Green Smoothie	Wednesday + Thursday
Fried Rice and Eggs	Friday
Zucchini Muffins and Herby Eggs	Saturday + Sunday

HEAD CHEF

_____

(Write your name here)

Imagine you are the head chef at your home for the week. What will you want on the menu for breakfast? Follow these rules for a balanced meal. Then write in your breakfast menu to the side.

☐ Include a protein like beans, tofu, eggs, yogurt, milk, soymilk, or nuts.

☐ Include at least one fruit or a whole grain.

☐ Include a healthy fat, like avocado, olive oil, or nuts.

Look at the Dinosaur Cereal Bites recipe on page 66. Write in the name of the ingredient that matches the food group. Some may be blank.

VEGGIES   FRUITS   GRAINS   DAIRY   PROTEIN   FATS

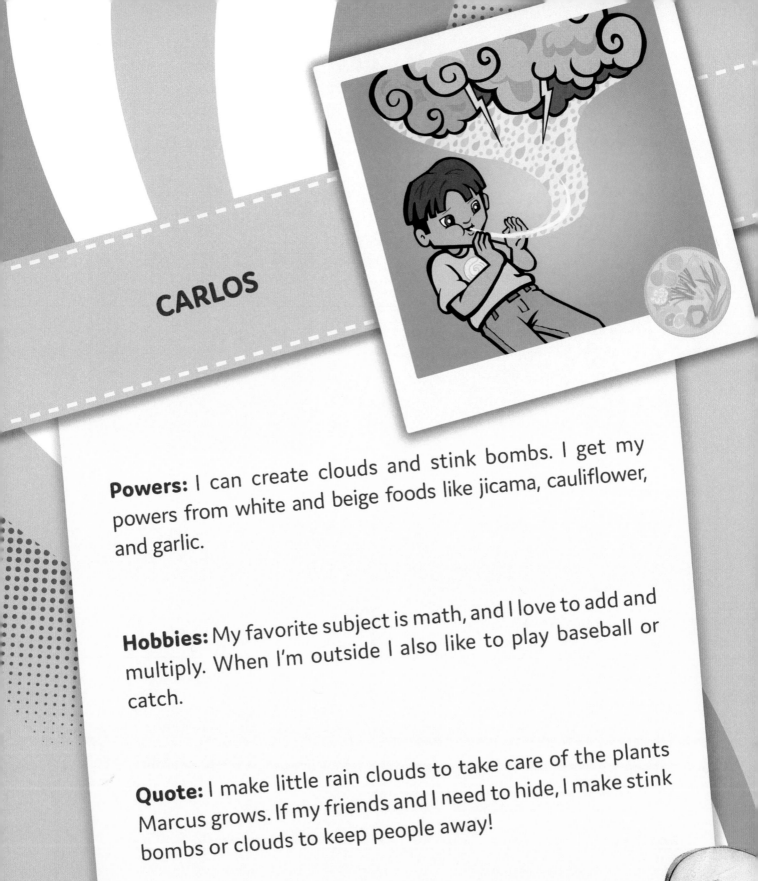

CARLOS

Powers: I can create clouds and stink bombs. I get my powers from white and beige foods like jicama, cauliflower, and garlic.

Hobbies: My favorite subject is math, and I love to add and multiply. When I'm outside I also like to play baseball or catch.

Quote: I make little rain clouds to take care of the plants Marcus grows. If my friends and I need to hide, I make stink bombs or clouds to keep people away!

COCONUT OVERNIGHT OATS

Makes 2-3 servings

Make these oats before you go to bed and breakfast will be ready when you wake up!

Ingredients:

- ½ cup whole old-fashioned oats
- ¾-1 cup skim milk or any milk alternative (add more if you like extra milky oats)
- ½ cup blueberries (fresh or frozen)
- 1 Tbsp. Greek yogurt
- 2 Tbsp. chopped nuts (roasted nuts or walnuts)
- 1 tsp. honey, maple syrup, or agave syrup
- 2 Tbsp. unsweetened shredded coconut
- *Optional:* ¼ tsp. cinnamon, ¼ tsp. vanilla extract

Directions:

1. Place all ingredients in a glass jar or a to-go-container with a lid.
2. Mix a few times and place in the refrigerator overnight.
3. In the morning, the oats will have soaked up the liquid and your breakfast will be ready!
4. Serve immediately and enjoy!

MINI BANANA WALNUT OAT PANCAKES WITH BERRIES

Makes 16 mini pancakes or
6-8 regular size waffles

Ingredients:

- 2 cups oat flour
- 4 tsp. GF baking powder
- ¼ tsp. salt
- 2 eggs
- 3 bananas, mashed (fresh or defrost a frozen banana)
- 1¾ cups milk of your choice
- ¼ cup canola oil
- 1 tsp. vanilla extract
- Crushed or whole walnuts (mix in batter or use as toppings)
- Maple syrup (pour in a small dish and dip your pancake)
- *Optional:* ⅓ tsp. cinnamon

Directions:

1. Mix all dry ingredients in a bowl.
2. Mix all wet ingredients in a separate bowl.
3. Mash a banana on a plate, then mix into wet ingredients.
4. Pour wet ingredients into dry ingredients and whisk until bubbly.
5. Lightly oil skillet if not using a non-stick variety, and heat skillet on medium-high heat.
6. Spoon small or large amounts of batter onto the skillet (depending on desired pancake size) or put the batter into a waffle maker.
7. Flip the pancakes when the top side and edges start to bubble.
8. Continue to cook until both sides are golden-brown and cooked through, then enjoy!

I love making these as waffles too. They really hit it out of the park! Try making them with a waffle maker.

RANCHERO TOFU

Makes 2 servings

Ingredients:

- 1 cup sprouted, soft or medium tofu
- ½ cup black beans
- 1 cup fresh spinach
- ¼ cup diced tomato
- 2 Tbsp. red onion
- 1 tsp. extra virgin olive oil
- ¼ avocado
- 4 tsp. salsa autentica (or salsa)
- ⅛ tsp. cumin
- ⅛ tsp. garlic powder
- Dash of salt and pepper
- 2 corn taco shells
- *Optional:* Shredded Mexican cheese

Directions:

1. Chop the red onion and place it in ice cold water. This removes the bitterness and brings out the sweetness.
2. Coat the pan with olive oil.
3. Let the kids crumble the tofu with their hands and place it in a pan with the black beans, tomatoes, spinach, salsa autentica, cumin and garlic. Sauté over medium-low heat for 3 minutes.
4. Drain the red onions and add them into the pan. Cook for 3-5 more minutes.
5. Serve with toasted corn taco shells and fresh avocado.

I love tofu! It's fun to cook because I can squish it with my hands!

I like using fresh or dried garlic and onion in my meals for extra flavor!

AMARANTH BREAKFAST PORRIDGE

Makes 2 servings

This delicious and nutritious twist on breakfast porridge is the perfect way to start your day!

Ingredients:

- 1 cup amaranth
- 2½ cups water
- ½-1 cup milk, soy milk or nut milk

Toppings per serving:
- 1 Tbsp. Greek Yogurt
- ¼-½ chopped pear
- 2 Tbsp. chopped nuts or pumpkin seeds
- 1 tsp. honey

Directions:

1. Place amaranth and water in a pot and bring to a boil.

2. Leaving the lid partially on, reduce the heat to a simmer and cook for 25-30 minutes, stirring occasionally.

3. Once all of the water has been soaked into the amaranth, gradually add in the milk until the desired consistency is reached. Your finished porridge will be slightly gelatinous.

4. To serve, pour into a bowl, top with your favorite porridge toppings, and enjoy!

TRY USING AMARANTH FLOUR FOR 1/4 OF THE FLOUR IN A RECIPE WHEN BAKING. IT HAS A NUTTY TASTE AND LOTS OF ANTIOXIDANTS.

ACTIVITY

OATS' SUPERPOWERS!

How many words can you make from **OATMEAL?**
Hint: There are over 30, some are two letter words.

Use another piece of paper to continue.

Carlos loves baseball! What activities do you like to do? List them below:

1. _____

2. _____

3. _____

Eating whole grains like oatmeal, whole-wheat, or amaranth gives me the energy to hit a home run!

Oats have two types of fiber:

- Soluble fiber helps lower cholesterol (kuh-les-tuh-rawl), a type of fat in your blood that you want to keep controlled.

- Insoluble fiber helps you poop!

Oats have a fight-o-nutrient called beta–glucan that lowers cholesterol. Try to say that 5 times fast!

TASTE EACH INGREDIENT!

Using your senses of taste, touch, sound, sight, and smell, write a description word next to each ingredient.

Examples: crunchy, sweet, bitter, bright, gooey, savory...

Oats _____

Berries _____

Nuts _____

Honey/Maple syrup _____

Coconut _____

TASTY TOPPINGS & TOFU

CARLOS' FAVORITE HOT CEREAL TOPPINGS!

Underline the toppings you like, and circle the ones you want to try. Then write in two of your own ideas!

- Bananas and tahini butter

- Greek yogurt, fresh or dried fruit and chopped nuts

- A few tablespoons of pumpkin purée (look for unsweetened), honey or maple syrup, cinnamon and walnuts

- A savory mix of fried egg, fresh chives and black pepper

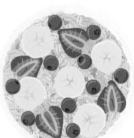

- _____

- _____

TOFU WORD SEARCH

Find some of the ways you can eat tofu in the word search. Highlight the ways you plan to try it!

K	S	M	A	A	T	H	C	P
E	E	A	Y	M	D	I	H	U
B	I	B	N	X	S	N	O	D
E	H	R	A	G	K	G	C	D
B	T	Q	R	B	A	T	O	I
F	O	L	C	H	S	S	L	N
M	O	U	S	S	E	V	A	G
W	M	A	G	J	F	S	T	L
L	S	Y	Z	I	U	N	E	A

Pudding   Smoothies
Lasagna   Chocolate
Kebabs   Mousse

Fill in the blanks to find the many types of tofu. Search for them with your parents at the grocery store. Circle the tofu you will try first this month!

Spiders spin it, and it's very soft: **L**   **K**   **N**
_ _ _ _ _ _

It's not hard, it's   **F**   **M**
_ _ _ _

This tofu has all the water removed: **P**   **R**   **D**
_ _ _ _ _ _

It has lots of flavor: **E**   **A**   **N**   **D**
_ _ _ _ _ _ _ _

BANANA TIPS

Here are the Super Crew's top banana tips.
Check off the one you want to try first!

☐ Instead of tossing banana peels into the trash, compost them! Toss them into your compost bin or cut them up into smaller pieces to add rich nutrients into your soil. They compost best in worm bins.

☐ If you feel like your banana is too ripe, don't throw it out! Store in the freezer to make banana bread or smoothies in the future.

☐ Need to speed up the ripening process? Put your banana in a paper bag with an apple, close the bag loosely, and store in a warmer area.

"What special key opens a banana?"

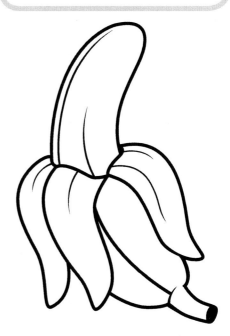

FIND THE NUTRIENTS IN CARLOS' BANANA!

V	F	A	P	E	D	V	W	O
I	I	S	O	O	F	I	B	F
G	B	T	T	U	T	T	A	C
N	E	S	A	Z	P	A	M	A
K	R	Y	S	M	F	M	S	X
P	S	E	S	A	I	I	V	R
S	J	V	I	Q	B	N	D	O
S	H	N	U	G	A	C	B	F
A	Q	I	M	W	E	E	R	H

Bananas are full of these nutrients:

fiber   vitamin B
potassium   vitamin C

ANDY

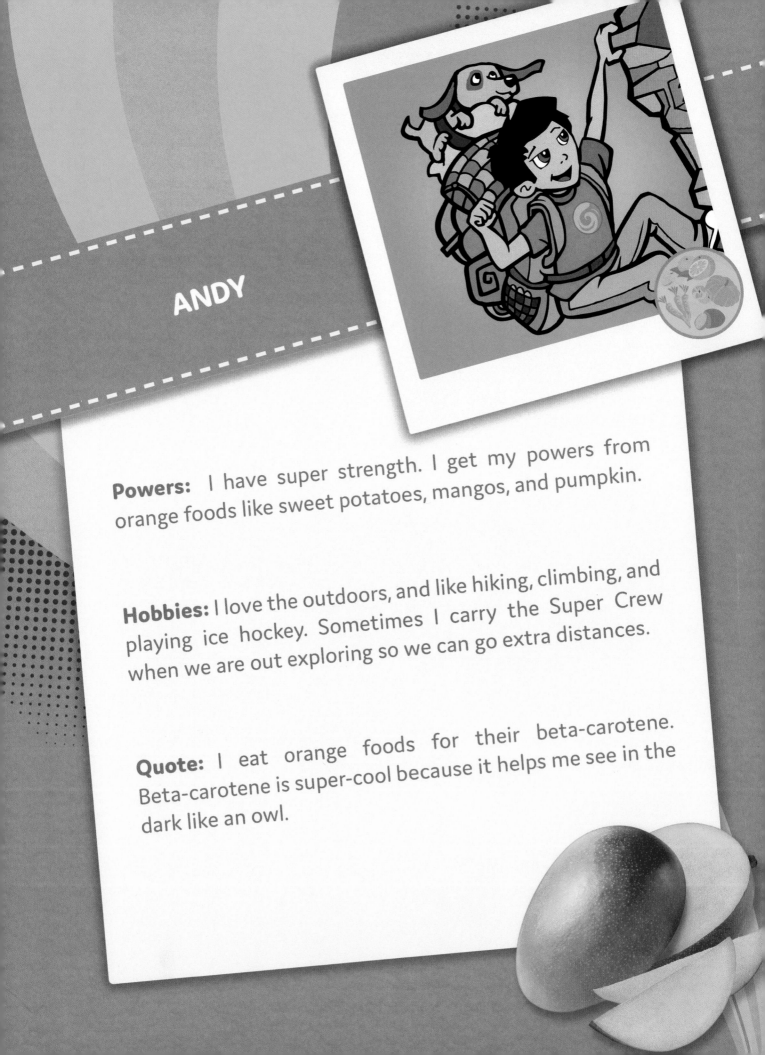

Powers: I have super strength. I get my powers from orange foods like sweet potatoes, mangos, and pumpkin.

Hobbies: I love the outdoors, and like hiking, climbing, and playing ice hockey. Sometimes I carry the Super Crew when we are out exploring so we can go extra distances.

Quote: I eat orange foods for their beta-carotene. Beta-carotene is super-cool because it helps me see in the dark like an owl.

SUPER PUMPKIN SMOOTHIE

Makes 1 serving

Ingredients:

- 1 ripe frozen banana, sliced
- ⅓ cup pumpkin purée
- ½ cup almond milk or cow's milk with ¼ tsp. almond extract
- ½ tsp. cinnamon
- *Optional:* ½ tsp. pumpkin pie spice

Directions:

1. Add all ingredients into a blender.
2. Blend until smooth.
3. Enjoy!

A LITTLE BIT OF CANNED PUMPKIN ADDS FLAVOR TO TOMATO SAUCE. IT'S ALSO DELICIOUS IN MUFFINS, COOKIES, AND OVERNIGHT OATS. PUMPKIN HAS NUTRIENTS THAT HELP GIVE YOUR SKIN THAT HEALTHY GLOW.

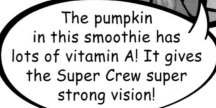

Pumpkin is a super food that isn't just for Fall! I like making this healthy pumpkin smoothie with my grandma all year round!

The pumpkin in this smoothie has lots of vitamin A! It gives the Super Crew super strong vision!

DRIED APRICOT GRANOLA

Makes about 8 cups

Make this big batch of granola over the weekend so you have some for a couple weeks. Store in an air tight container. It tastes great tossed in with your Greek yogurt!

Ingredients:

- 5 cups oats
- 4 oz. pecans
- 6 oz. almonds
- 5 oz. cranberries
- ½ cup organic coconut flakes
- ¾ cup dried apricots chopped
- ½ tsp. cinnamon
- 1½ Tbsp. canola oil
- ½ tsp. vanilla extract
- 2½ tsp. honey

Directions:

1. Mix all of the dry ingredients into a bowl.
2. Pour oil over the ingredients and toss, then mix in the honey and vanilla extract. Sprinkle with cinnamon.
3. Bake at 300°F for 15 minutes, then toss and bake for another 15 minutes.
4. Let cool before storing.

I make a big batch of this recipe with my dad and store it in an air tight container.

I like eating this granola on top of Greek yogurt for breakfast before we go rock climbing!

HEARTY FARMERS MARKET SCONES

Makes 6 scones

*For gluten-free swap out whole-wheat flour for almond flour and increase chia seeds to 2 Tbsp.

Ingredients:

- 1 ripe banana
- ¾ cup apple, grated (about one small apple)
- 1 cup zucchini, grated (about one medium zucchini)
- 1 cup carrot, grated (about one medium carrot)
- ¼ cup raisins
- 1 tsp. ginger, fresh grated
- 1 Tbsp. vegetable oil
- 1 egg, beaten
- 1 Tbsp. chia seeds*
- ¼ cup almond milk
- 1½ cups whole-wheat flour*
- 1 cup rolled oats
- ½ tsp. cinnamon
- 1 tsp. baking soda
- ⅛ tsp. salt
- ¼ cup of your favorite types of seeds or chopped nuts
- *Optional*: Dark chocolate baking chips or chunks

Directions:

1. Preheat the oven to 375°F.
2. Lightly oil a baking sheet, line with parchment paper or use silicone baking mat.
3. In a small bowl, combine the chia seeds with the almond milk and set aside.
4. In a medium bowl, mash the banana and combine with the remaining wet ingredients.
5. In a separate bowl, combine the dry ingredients and mix well.
6. Mix in the wet ingredients (including your chia mixture) into the dry and mix until just combined.
7. Shape into rounded scones and place on the baking sheet. Bake for about 20 minutes, or until a toothpick inserted into the center comes out clean.
8. Remove from the oven, let cool, and enjoy!

These scones give me energy to get outdoors and play! My mom likes that this recipe is packed with fruits and vegetables. I like the nutty crunch!

ANDY'S CLEMENTINE FRENCH TOAST

Makes 2 servings

Ingredients:

French Toast
- 1 egg
- ¼ cup low-fat or nonfat milk or milk alternative
- 2 slices whole-grain bread
- Canola or olive oil to coat the pan

Toppings
- 2-3 Tbsp. Greek yogurt (low-fat plain or flavored)
- 2 fresh clementines, peeled and separated
- 1 tsp. cinnamon
- ⅛ tsp. zest from clementine (zest is the outer peel)
- Several drops of vanilla or almond extract
- Drizzle of honey or maple syrup

Directions:

1. In a wide shallow bowl, whisk together the egg and milk alternative.
2. One at a time, soak the bread until well saturated, making sure both sides are fully coated.
3. Grill your soaked bread in a skillet coated with olive oil over medium heat.
4. Flip half-way through, cooking until both sides are a lovely golden brown.
5. Prepare Greek yogurt topping by combining the yogurt, cinnamon, and vanilla or almond extract in a small bowl and mixing well. Spread this over your cooked French toast, then top each piece with fresh clementines and extra honey or maple syrup if desired.
6. Enjoy!

This breakfast has a tasty zing. Clementines are loaded with vitamin C!

They help my immune system stay strong so I stay healthy for soccer!

WHOLE GRAIN SMOOTHIE BOWL

Makes 3-4 servings

Ingredients:

- 2 cups frozen mango, chopped
- ½ cup nonfat Greek yogurt
- ½ cup milk (cow or plant-based)
- ½-1 Tbsp. honey
- 6-10 raspberries
- 2 Tbsp. toasted almond slices
- 1 cup healthy cereal (like Andy's granola, puffed brown rice, or amaranth)
- Dash of cinnamon

Directions:

1. In a blender, add together the mango, yogurt, milk, and honey. Blend well until smooth.
2. Pour smoothie mixture into a bowl and top off with raspberries.
3. Arrange almond slices and healthy cereal on top.
4. Sprinkle a dash of cinnamon over your smoothie bowl.
5. Enjoy for breakfast or a refreshing dessert.

3 GRAB-N-GO BREAKFAST RECIPES

Some mornings I have to eat breakfast on the way to school. Here are my tasty and healthy favorites!

Directions: Draw in the missing foods.

Breakfast 1:

- Clementines
- Whole-wheat crackers
- String cheese

+ ⬚ + ⬚

Breakfast 2:

- Kefir milk or box milk
- Andy's granola

+ ⬚

Breakfast 3:

- Soy milk
- Apple or dried apricots
- Granola bar

+ ⬚

WORD GUESSING GAME

Can you unscramble five of the ingredients that Andy needs to make his Dried Apricot Granola recipe on page 84?

1. ECNASP   __ __ __ __ __ __

2. AAILNLV   __ __ __ __ __ __ __

3. ONAMLSD   __ __ __ __ __ __ __

4. TASO   __ __ __ __

5. OYHEN   __ __ __ __ __

FILL IN THE BLANKS
Can you guess 3 of my favorite orange foods?

E   A
__ __ __ __ __ __ __ __ __ __

C   E
__ __ __ __ __ __ __

U   K
__ __ __ __ __ __

BALANCING YOUR MEALS

What makes a balanced breakfast? Carbohydrate, protein and healthy fat!

Smoothie Bowl Base

- ☐ Greek yogurt (protein)
- ☐ Cow's milk, kefir, soy milk (protein)
- ☐ Fresh or frozen fruit (carbohydrate)

Topping Your Smoothie Bowl

Check off what you want to try on top of your smoothie bowl:

- ☐ Flax meal (healthy fat)
- ☐ Granola (carbohydrate)
- ☐ Crushed peanuts (healthy fat)
- ☐ Cocoa powder (carbohydrate)
- ☐ Chopped apple (carbohydrate)
- ☐ Chia seeds (healthy fat)
- ☐ Puffed whole-grain cereal (carbohydrate)

Citrus fruits like oranges, lemons and limes have lots of vitamin C that are good for healthy gums, which support healthy teeth.

ANDY'S CITRUS TIPS

Citrus fruit and juices give a flavor boost to many dishes. What's your favorite type of citrus fruits? Write or draw them in below.

Color in the vitamin C molecule below with the different colors of citrus fruits.

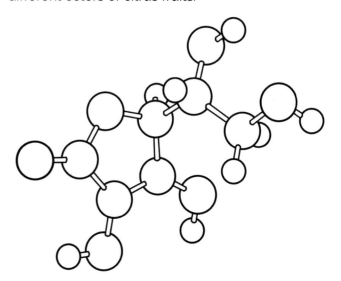

THE SUPER CREW'S FOOD RIDDLE FUN!

Directions: Solve each of the riddles. Then on a separate piece of paper, make up your own, and have your family guess the answer. Use the coloring images as inspiration!

I'm green on the outside and red with black accents on the inside. I can help keep you hydrated on hot summer days. I taste great as fruit, or blended as a drink. I'm Super Crew kid Tom-Tom's favorite fruit.

WHAT AM I? _____

I'm green and leafy and Jessie loves me. I come as an adult or baby. Sometimes I'm hidden in smoothies and you can't taste me, but usually I'm cooked up or eaten in salads. Some people say I make you strong.

WHAT AM I? _____

I'm sweet and juicy and wear my seeds on the outside. I'm popular in summer, but also on Valentine's day. Will you be my Valentine?

WHAT AM I? _____

I come fresh or dried, and have a pit inside. Andy loves me in his homemade granola.

WHAT AM I? _____

My skin is dark green and my insides are light green and yellow. I have a big seed inside of me. I am creamy and high in heart-healthy fats and potassium. I'm tasty in breakfast omelets with beans and salsa. I'm one of Super Crew kid Jessie's favorite foods!

WHAT AM I? _____

THE SUPER CREW'S COLORING PAGE

Color the image and write in your own message!

THE SUPER CREW'S BODY POWER BINGO

Directions: Complete any row of the activities to get a body power boost! Draw a heart around each activity you complete, since they're good for your heart. After achieving a completed row, decide with your parents what your reward for BINGO will be! Positive reward examples include reading a book together, playing catch, cooking with a parent, seeing a new movie, going to the farmers market or playground, getting a hug, a small toy, or a sticker!

I completed the Purple Power Foods word search.	I exercised today!	I tried a new breakfast recipe.	I tried a new whole grain.	I helped clean the kitchen after eating.
I created my own smoothie!	I helped make a recipe.	I learned a new nutrition fact or tip.	I found Pinkie the fish 3 times.	I tried a new food!
I tried a new green food!	I tried pumpkin or pumpkin seeds.	Freebie	I exercised today!	I measured an ingredient for a recipe.
I finished Kira's Whole Grain Fun activity.	I can name one of the Super Crew kids' superpowers.	I went to the farmers market.	I ate a fresh, frozen, or canned fruit today.	I found Cinnamon the dog 3 times.
I colored in a healthy food.	I tried a new recipe!	I learned a fact about bees.	I helped make breakfast.	I completed the Eat Your Water activity.

EAT THEIR COLOR POWER FOODS

Directions: In the space below, draw 3 different plant-based foods you'll eat today! Then circle the color hearts based on the colors you ate. If the color isn't there, color in the empty heart.

Eat more healthy foods to feel better, run faster, jump higher and think your best!

ACTIVITY

SET GOALS TO FEEL & LIVE YOUR BEST

#1: Write a tasty way to reach your goal to eat more brown foods below. Fill in the food group where your food choice fits, and describe what it will do for your body.

Kira's **Example:** Brown foods

"Today I am going to add a few **walnuts** (a healthy fat) to my yogurt to boost my brain power"

YOUR TURN:

I am going to eat _____

to _____.

#2: Write a tasty way to reach your goal to eat more orange foods below:

Andy's **Example:** Orange foods

"I am going to try a new **orange** food like **papaya** at the farmers market this weekend."

YOUR TURN:

I am going to try _____

_____

#3: Write a tasty way to reach your goal to eat more green foods below:

Jessie's **Example:** Green foods

"This week instead of butter I'm going to try mashed **avocado** on my toast with **lime** and **herbs**."

YOUR TURN:

This week _____

_____.

P.13 Help Super Baby Abigail Get Through the Eye Maze!

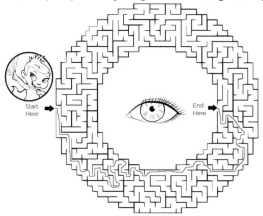

Answer to vitamin family: Vitamin A

P.14 The Super Crew's Super Smoothie
Answers for matching Super Crew kids to their powers:
Marcus = lemon juice; Andy = mango, peach in kefir milk;
Carlos = unsalted cashews, oats; Tom-Tom = raspberries

P.24 Kira's Whole Grain Fun - Whole Grain Unscramble
Answers:

Popcorn	Quinoa
Brown rice	Barley
Oatmeal	Spelt
Farro	Whole-wheat

P.25 Check Your Knowledge on Whole Grains
True Statements:
Whole grains have fiber.
Whole grains have vitamins.
Whole grains can taste good.
Whole grains have antioxidants.
Whole grains help you poop.

P.26 Kira's Favorite Ways to Eat Whole Grains
Answers: FIBER, VITAMINS, HEART or BRAIN

P.28 Can You Crack the Code?
Answers: CINNAMON STICKS, SORGHUM

P.33 Bee Fun

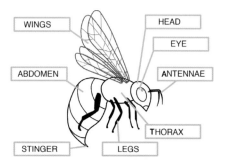

Riddle Answer: He finally found his honey.

P.35 Playing Detective!
Answers:

YESTERDAY	YUCCA
YOGA	YARD

Answer for Let's Play a Game: there are several variations but only one winner. The person who starts first, always wins.

P.41 What Do You BEE-lieve?
Answers for: Which honey bee facts do you think are true?: 1. T 2. F – five eyes 3. T 4. T 5. F – only a few types including the honey bee 6. T 7. T

P.42 Penny's Purple Foods
Answer for Why does Penny like purple grapes?: ANTIOXIDANTS
Purple foods: Currants, mulberry, passion fruits, purple cabbage, purple grapes, purple figs, purple rice, purple potatoes, purple cornmeal

P.43 Guess What's Different

P.45 Super Baby Abigail's Parfait Fun!
Riddle Answer: Blood orange

P.51 Eat Your Water with Tom-Tom!
Answers for Circle the foods that come in Tom-Tom's favorite color red:
Strawberries, Watermelon, Tomatoes, Radishes, Grapefruit
Answers for starred 5 foods with highest amount of water (high to low):
Lettuce, Radishes, Cucumbers, Tomatoes, Watermelon
Answers for measuring cup activity: 32 tablespoons; will vary based on watermelon consistency, (subtract the difference between the watermelon pieces and juice for fun)
Answers for liquid measurements: 16 tablespoons; 32 tablespoons

P.53 Word Play Answers for word play: aim, am,

amino, an, anion, cam, camo, can, cannon, coin, coma, con, icon, in, inn, ion, main, man, manic, no, on

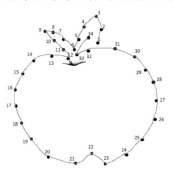

P.70 Jessie's Math Riddles
Answers:

AVOCADO	BROCCOLI
CILANTRO	GRAPES

Answers: CORE, 1 + 14 + 11 + 4 = 30

P.72 Jessie's Green Food Guessing Game
Answers: pear, kiwi, cashew
Answer for number of pods: 11 (eleven)

P.73 Food Groups and Your Menu with Jessie

Veggies	Fruits	Grains
spinach	applesauce	oat flour

Dairy	Protein	Fats
-	eggs	olive oil

P.79 Oats' Superpowers – How many words can you make from OATMEAL?
Answers: aloe, am, at, ate, eat, elm, lame, late, let, lot, male, malt, mat, mate, meal, meat, melt, met, metal, moat, mole, molt, motel, oat, tale, tamale, tame, tea, teal, team, to, toe

P.80 Carlos' Tasty Toppings & Tofu - Tofu Word Search

K	S	M	A	A	T	H	C	P
E	E	A	Y	M	D	I	H	U
B	I	B	N	X	S	N	O	D
E	H	R	A	G	K	G	C	D
B	T	Q	R	B	A	T	O	I
F	O	L	C	H	S	S	L	N
M	O	U	S	S	E	V	A	G
W	M	A	G	J	F	S	T	L
L	S	Y	Z	I	U	N	E	A

Answers to fill in the blank: silken, firm, pressed, seasoned

P.81 Banana Tips
Riddle Answer: a monkey

V	F	A	P	E	D	V	W	O
I	I	S	O	O	F	I	B	F
G	B	T	T	U	T	T	A	C
N	E	S	A	Z	P	A	M	A
K	R	Y	S	M	F	M	S	X
P	S	E	S	A	I	I	V	R
S	J	V	I	Q	B	N	D	O
S	H	N	U	G	A	C	B	F
A	Q	I	M	W	E	E	R	H

P.89 Andy's Word Guessing Game
Answers for the unscramble: 1. pecans 2. vanilla 3. almonds 4. oats 5. honey
Answers for the fill in the blanks: sweet potato, cantaloupe or clementine, pumpkin

P.91 The Super Crew's Food Riddle Fun!
Answers: watermelon, spinach or kale, strawberry, apricot, avocado

Animal/Pet Count
Cinnamon the Dog: 23
Pinkie the Fish: 19
Quack Duck: 15
Flutter the Butterfly: 20

MELISSA'S NUTRITION PHILOSOPHY

Food should be enjoyed and cherished. It nourishes our bodies, elicits our senses, and is often shared amongst family and friends with good conversation and love. How we eat is just as important as what we eat. Getting your kids to explore cooking with you at an early age can help them gain independence, self-reliance, and healthy habits. Cooking together creates life-long memories that are passed on through generations of healthy eaters.

Making healthy eating a part of your family's life may take more effort in the beginning, but it gets easier as it becomes part of the fabric of your home. You get into a rhythm, and what once seemed like a hurdle, becomes a habit.

Growing up with a tasty kitchen and learning how to cook with my mom has been one of the greatest joys I've passed on to my little girl. It's also a source of happiness to see friends and family gathered around my table, enjoying the food I prepared for them with love. Experimenting with new foods and flavors, cooking with children, and growing food with my daughter in our garden continues to feed my love for nutrition!

ABOUT MELISSA

Melissa Halas, MA, RDN, CDE is a Registered Dietitian Nutritionist, Certified Diabetes Educator, and wellness expert. She has a passion for making good nutrition come to life for kids through hands-on learning and tasty inspiration, which led to the creation of SuperKidsNutrition.com and the Super Crew®.

When Melissa first became a mom, she was surprised to find limited expert resources on childhood nutrition. SuperKids Nutrition Inc. and the Super Crew were her solution. In 2006, SuperKidsNutrition.com was the first premier source and mega site for kids' and family nutrition. The Super Crew is a group of multi-cultural characters who get their powers from healthy plant-based foods and help motivate young children to develop healthy eating habits from an early age. The Super Crew has been focus group tested and is kid and parent approved. The characters appear on thousands of school websites across the US and in health curriculum through partnerships with national organizations to drive healthier change. Once kids dive into the Super Crew's world through Melissa's children's books and activities, good nutrition will take on a whole new meaning. Healthy eating has never been so fun!

Melissa has 20 years of diverse experience in nutrition care, including childhood nutrition, nutrition counseling, curriculum development, functional foods, sports nutrition, clinical trials, media, and writing. Melissa is the parent nutrition expert for the People.com online magazine and a past panel expert on Childhood Obesity for TedMed. She provides nutrition counseling through Melissa's Healthy Living to help clients of all ages reach their best health!